DOM MANUEL II
The last King of Portugal:
His life and reign

by Malcolm Howe

The Foundation of the Order of Saint Michael of the Wing
established in the United Kingdom, in the year of Our Lord 1984

ISBN nº 0-9540023-2-6

Depósito Legal nº 293457/09 Reservados todos os direitos em Portugal

Michaelmas 2009
500 copies
Production by: Book Press 4 Maclise Road, London W14 0PR

Dedicated to the memory of Dr Hilary Standish-Barry (1953-91)
Honorary Knight of the Order of St. Michael of the Wing
who received the accolade bestowed by His Royal Highness the Duke of Braganza
on 1st June 1986

Front cover: Drawing by Bernard Partridge, leading illustrator of *Punch*, featured in
the 12th February 1908 issue, depicting *Britannia*, with her trident reversed in
mourning, admonishing the eighteen year old new King purposely armed as a knight

It gives me great pleasure to write the foreword to this work about King Manuel ll of Portugal by Malcolm Howe. As well as drawing on research he has already undertaken about the Portuguese Royal Family the author also brings to the English speaking public for the first time the King's own account of the assassination of his father King Carlos and his brother Crown Prince Luís in 1908. As the author vividly demonstrates, the King and his mother narrowly escaped death at the same time.

King Manuel was a tragic figure thrust into high office at a young age and who reigned but two years before being forced into exile. This exile was to be the gain of St James's Church, where he regularly attended mass with his wife Queen Augusta. The King and Queen were generous benefactors of the parish, and godparents to countless children when the latter received the Sacrament of Confirmation. They worked closely with my predecessor Canon Michael English, who was Parish Priest for much of the seventeen years when King Manuel was a parishioner at St James's. The two fine stained glass windows at the front of the church were donated by the King in memory of Canon English. Although the King's life was beset with much sadness he remained a devout Catholic and also sought to support his homeland from which he had been so unjustly exiled. In particular he was assiduous in lending succour to the Portuguese divisions sent to serve on the Western Front in horrendous conditions during the First World War.

The publication of this book coincides with the installation of a memorial to King Manuel. Such a commemoration is long overdue and our parish is extremely grateful to the Order of St Michael of the Wing for their generosity by enhancing our church in this fine way.

I commend to you this excellent work. Portugal's loss was St James's gain.

Introduction

To mark the silver jubilee of the establishment in the United Kingdom of the Portuguese Order of St Michael of the Wing, it is appropriate to celebrate Michaelmas at the Church of St James, Strawberry Hill, Twickenham, where the last King of Portugal worshipped in exile in England. Although still remembered as godparents and generous benefactors, the church lacks any memorial to Dom Manuel II and his Queen. The Foundation of the Order in the United Kingdom is pleased to rectify this by bearing the costs of a marble inscribed tablet. The Braganza Story published in 1999 has been out of print for several years. Hence it was decided to re-issue the section and illustrations relating to Dom Manuel with appropriate additions, including for the first time an English translation of Dom Manuel's own account of the Regicide.

THE ROYAL HOUSE OF BRAGANZA : FAMILY TREE 3   DONA MARIA II - DOM MANUEL II   THE CONSTITUTIONAL SOVEREIGNS OF PORTUGAL

Dom AUGUSTO de Beauharnais
1810-35
cr HRH Prince of Portugal,
Duke of Santa Cruz in Brazil
s of HI &RH Prince Eugene de Beauharnais,
1st Duke of Leuchtenberg, Prince of
Eichstadt, adopted by the Emperor Napoleon
I, & Augusta, d of Maximilian I King of
Bavaria

m1
1835
no issue

Dona MARIA II da Glória
1819-53

2m
1836

Dom FERNANDO II
1816-85
King Consort 1837,
Regent 1853-55, s of Duke
Ferdinand of Saxe-Coburg
& Gotha & Antonia, d of
Franz Josef, Prince of
Kohary

Elise Frederica Hensler
1836-1929
cr Countess von Edla by
Duke of Saxe-Coburg &
Gotha, d of Joseph Hensler
& Josepha Hechelbacher

2m
morganatic
1869
no issue

Dom PEDRO V
1837-61

m
1858
no issue

Dona ESTEFÂNIA
1837-59
d of Karl Anton
Prince of
Hohenzollern-
Sigmaringen &
Josephine d of Karl,
Grand Duke of Baden

Dom LUÍS I
1838-89
Duke of
Oporto until
accession

m
1862

Dona Maria Pia
de Sabóia (of Savoy)
1847-1911
d of Vittorio Emanuele II King of Italy &
Adelaide, d of HI & RH Archduke Rainer
of Austria, Viceroy of Lombardo-
Venetian Kingdom & Elizabetta, d of
Carlo Emanuele, Prince of Savoy-
Carignano

Dona Maria
b & †
10 Oct, 1840

Dom JOÃO
1842-61
Duke of Beja

Dona Maria Ana
1843-84

m
1859
George I,
King of
Saxony
1832-1904

issue &
present Royal
Family of
Saxony

Dona Antónia
1845-1913

m
1861
Leopold, Prince
of Hohenzollern
1835-1905

issue &
present
Roumanian
Royal Family

See Family Tree 6 showing Links
Braganza/Hohenzollern/Roumania

Dom FERNANDO
1846-61

Dom AUGUSTO
1847-89
Duke of Coimbra

Dom LEOPOLDO
b & †
7 May, 1849

Dona MARIA
da Glória
b & † 3 Feb,
1851

Dom EUGÉNIO*
MARIA
b & † 15 Nov,
1853
*NB According to
inscription on
tomb: D. Eugénia

D. Fernando II   D. Maria II   D. Pedro V   D. Luís I   D. Carlos I   D. Manuel II

Dom CARLOS I*
1863-1908§

m
1886

Dona AMÉLIA
1865-1951
d of Prince Louis Philippe of Orleans, Count of Paris &
Marie Isabelle, Infanta of Spain, d of Prince Antoine,
Duke of Montpensier & the Infanta Luísa Fernanda, d of
King Fernando VII of Spain & sister of Queen Isabel II
of Spain

Dom AFONSO
1865-1920
Duke of Oporto
Heir Presumptive 1910-20

Nevada Stoody Hayes
1870-1941
b Sandyville Ohio, USA
Sarah Nevada Stoody d
of Jacob Walter Stoody
& Nancy d of James
Powell McNeil
† Tampa, Florida, USA

m4
1917
no issue

Philip van Valkenburgh
1854-1949

3m
1909
div 1917

William Henry Chapman
1830-1907

2m
1906

Lee A.
Agnew
1868-1924

1m
1897
div 1906

Dona Augusta Vitória
1890-1966
d of Wilhelm, Prince of
Hohenzollern & Maria
Theresa Madgalena d of
Prince Lodovico of
Bourbon Two Sicilies

m1
1913
no issue

Robert, 9th Count
Douglas
1880-1955
s of Ludwig, 8th Count
Douglas, Riksmarskalk-
Marshal of the Royal
Court of Sweden & Anna,
d of Albert, 5th Count
Ehrensvard

2m
1939
no issue

Sophia
d of Professor
Soloman de
Fineblaauw

m1
1906

→ issue

Dom LUÍS FILIPE*
1887-1908§
Prince of Beira until his
father's accession
Príncipe Real
(Crown Prince)

Dona MARIA
Ana
b & † 14 Dec, 1888

Dom MANUEL II
1889-1932
Duke of Beja
until accession
† Twickenham

*Both styled Duke of
Braganza on coming of age

§ Both assassinated
1st February, 1908

Queen Maria Pia with her elder son
Carlos; the drawing below shows Carlos
stopping a runaway horse during a visit
to London

Republicanism in Portugal :

During the last half of the 19th Century, the economy of Portugal had floundered, with a deficit equal to half the revenue and a national debt that absorbed half that revenue. Between 1868 and 1870 there were no less than nine different Ministers of Finance. Five London Jewish bankers received Portuguese titles of nobility for raising international loans. National bankruptcy led to the abandonment of the gold standard in Portugal in 1891 with the paper currency reaching a maximum depreciation of 37% by 1898. Unfortunately the Royal Family were targeted to be criticised as an unnecessary extravagance by the republican movement that gained ground from the 1870s onwards. The seeds of Portuguese republicanism were cultivated by anti-clerical intellectuals at Coimbra University[1] , rather than by the ordinary folk or peasants in a mainly illiterate country. Their cause did not start as a people's party with popular support but was well organised by the Freemasons, disaffected with the Constitutional Monarchy that their forebears had instituted in Portugal.

Moreover Portugal had suffered greatly from the ravages of three Napoleonic invasions during the Peninsular War, the loss of Brazil and subsequently the civil war, known as the *War of the two brothers*. When King John VI died in 1826, he was succeeded by his eldest son Dom Pedro, who had declared the independence of Brazil in 1822, As the reigning Emperor of Brazil, Dom Pedro abdicated the throne of Portugal in favour of his seven year old daughter Maria da Glória. Furthermore she was to be married to his younger brother Dom Miguel, age twenty-three, who would be Regent. In 1828 Dom Miguel was acclaimed King of Portugal but opposed by the Liberals many of whom were Freemasons. Dom Pedro was forced to abdicate the throne of Brazil in 1832 and led the Liberal forces which invaded Portugal and defeated his brother's army in 1834. Dom Miguel went into exile, died in 1866, but still had many loyal supporters ; hence the Portuguese Monarchists were of divided allegiance.

The reigning King Luís had two sons; the two brother princes Carlos and Afonso enjoyed a boisterous boyhood and with less than two years between them were the best of pals. Afonso, when chastised by his father for his pranks, used to shout *Viva a República !* At nine and eight years old respectively, their lives were saved from drowning in the Bay of Cascais by António de Almeida Neves, the lighthouse keeper at Mexilhoeira. Carlos was a talented painter, whose exhibited works won prizes and are widely admired and frequently reproduced in Portugal today. He was also a sculptor, an intellectual who loved drama, patronising female exponents of the theatre and he spoke seven languages, helping his father in his translation of Shakespeare's works into Portuguese.

1- Students' hostels are known as *Repúblicas* in Portuguese.

5

He was a diligent investigator in the field of oceanography, plumbing the depths from the Royal Yacht, which was equipped with a laboratory, charting the seas off the coast of Portugal and publishing learned works of his findings.

Afonso took a precocious interest in mechanics, joined the fire brigade at the Ajuda Palace, and rescued many from danger when the Chiado suffered a similar fire disaster to the more recent catastrophe. He introduced the first motor cars to Portugal and drove furiously through the Lisbon streets, shouting at the startled passers-by to get out of the way[2]. He repaired his vehicles himself in his own workshops.

Both princes were talented sportsmen and experienced bullfighters. Afonso could drive a chariot, controlling six horses and Carlos once fought a bull with horns unpadded, contrary to Portuguese custom.

In London Carlos stopped a runaway horse[3] and in Portugal he thrashed a footpad on the highway. Innumerable stories were told of the skills of Carlos as a marksman for example he could toss a stone in the air, split it with a shot from his revolver and then shatter a fragment with a second shot before the remains reached the ground; he hit a running deer a hundred yards away whilst riding a fast pony; he potted fish on the lake at Óbidos as they rose to the surface; with a vertical shot; he brought down an eagle, flying eighty yards overhead. How ironic that he was destined to die from an assassin's shot in the back of the neck at point blank range!

When twenty-two in 1886, Carlos chose as his bride Princess Amélia , daughter of the Head of the French Royal Family, Prince Louis Philippe of Orleans[4] . The Portuguese people adored her because although she was a large lady, she was accomplished, charming, kind and remarkably brave. In 1888 she rescued her first born Luís Filipe from a blazing cradle at Vila Viçosa but the shock brought on the premature arrival of her second child; sadly this daughter died at birth.

Amélia visited plague-stricken hospitals, founded the first tuberculosis dispensary and Pasteur Institute in Portugal and brought the first phials of anti-diphtheria serum from Paris to Lisbon. No mere honorary patron, she actually organised many charitable institutions and presided over committee meetings.

2- From these antics Afonso became nicknamed *O Arreda* = the one from whom you needed to move back, as startled pedestrians shouted out *Wo ! Slow down* more succinctly translated as *The Speedy.*

3- The incident is said to have happened in The Mall. Carlos Place in Mayfair was so named in 1886 to commemorate his marriage.

4 - Grandson of King Louis Philippe of France, who reigned 1830-48 (god-father of King Luís of Portugal) and first cousin of Prince Gaston, who had married Isabel, Princess Imperial of Brazil.

Achieving this without any funds from the State, the poor of the nation were indebted to her noble works. When she saw a fisherman in difficulties she plunged without hesitation into the sea, fully clothed and rescued him from drowning. Deeply religious, she became a close confidant of the Count-Bishop of Coimbra and they regularly corresponded[5]. Her support for the re-establishment of the religious orders in Portugal did not endear the Queen to the school of anti-clerical reform centred on the republicans.

The end of the Constitutional Monarchy in Portugal:

1889 saw the accession of Carlos, the birth of his second son Manuel, on 15th November, the same day that the Braganza Monarchy in Brazil was deposed and the nadir of Anglo-Portuguese relations. The Treaty of Windsor had endured by then five hundred years but the most ancient unbroken alliance between nations nearly ended with the infamous ultimatum from Great Britain to Portugal. This arose over alleged infringements of colonial rights in Africa. Portugal sought the expansion of Mozambique and Angola, which England saw as a threat to the South Africa of the British Empire. The British Government issued an ultimatum in 1890 and the Portuguese government backed down in an unpopular move to avoid conflict. This was opposed by the republicans who were now seen as patriots.

The Royal Family were criticised for being pro-British and there were demonstrations and insurrections. In 1890 Alfredo Keil composed a grand tune *The Portuguese Girl = A Portuguesa* and the republicans adopted it with stirring words as their rallying song. Sung at demonstrations against the infamous British ultimatum, the chorus rang out *To arms! To arms! To fight for the Country! To march against the Britons, to march!*[6]

A republican uprising in Oporto on 31st January 1891 was put down with brutality and supporters driven into exile. It was impossible to avert national bankruptcy in 1891. Tight press censorship was imposed and by 1901 the intellectual republican party was excluded from parliament. Nevertheless the republicans gained control of Lisbon.

5- Her letters to the Count-Bishop from 1893 to 1913 were published, in Lisbon in 1948.

6- *Às armas! Às armas! Pela Pátria lutar! Contra os Bretões, marchar, marchar!* However when it was adopted as the National Anthem in 1911 ousting the former Constitutional Monarchist anthem, the words were replaced by *To march against the cannons, to march: Contra os canões, marchar, marchar!* Words by Henrique Lopes de Mendoça.

Manuel, aged six, with his elder brother Luis Filipe, aged eight, in 1895; Manuel aged ten, dressed in the costume of a traditional attendant in a Bullfight procession, at a children's fancy dress party at Sintra in 1899. The two brothers, growing up, in formal day dress and their signatures in 1907 when Luís was nineteen and Manuel seventeen.

The Portuguese political system had become rotational whereby successive politicians in power took it in turns to cut up what was left of the crumbling cake and enjoy the diminishing slices. Carlos expressed his views as follows: *I can change nothing in this condition of things, for no responsible Minister and no parliament which one could get elected would lend itself to the measures required to put an end to the scandal. Ah! If only I could find a really honest man - a patriot who would put the honour and interest of Portugal before his personal interests and those of his adherents! How gladly and gratefully would I support such a man with all the power at my command! How willingly would I delegate to him all the authority which I have in order that he might introduce the era of reform which I and the Portuguese people equally desire.* It sounded a noble utterance and Carlos believed he had fulfilled these wishes when in 1906 he installed his nominee Franco[7], with dictatorial powers.

However Carlos had not learned that those who live in glass houses should not throw stones. The Civil List of £112,000 per year was overdrawn by £154,000 and Franco agreed that the solution to this indebtedness was for the King to sell to the nation by Royal decree the Royal Yacht and some unused property at inflated prices. The King's annual allowance was then increased by £32,000 but the anti-monarchical Press exposed these unwise moves. This provided considerable ammunition for the republicans. There arose a surging tide of popular resentment against the King on account of his dictatorial regime and especially the doubtful financial administration. Government commissioners were appointed to control the hitherto autonomous municipal authorities. The republicans protested with vigour and there were repeated extremely serious street tumults in Lisbon. An attempted coup to seize the Ministry of the Interior and establish telegraphic control of the country failed on the 28th January 1908 and ninety-three republican suspects were imprisoned.

----

7 - João Ferreira **Franco** Pinto Castelo Branco (1855-1929) graduated in Law from Coimbra University 1875, deputy 1884 Regeneration Party, highly critical of Progressive Party governments, Minister of the Exchequer 1890, Public Works 1891-92 & of the Realm 1893-97, left the Regeneration Party to form in 1903 the Liberal Regeneration Centre; President of the Council & Minister of the Realm 19 May 1906-4 February 1908, allowing the creation of a criminal revolutionary environment. It was reputed that he was so concerned there would be an attempt on his life he always slept at a different address each night and after the assassination he took refuge in the quarters of the Civil Governor of Lisbon in the Chiado. On 4th February he was dismissed from office by Dom Manuel and seen crying like a child, as he left the Palace. Soon after he left Portugal, abandoned his political career, saying that the assassinations were a black page in history but he did not propose to be the historian.

Queen Alexandra, with Queen Amélia and the Queen Mother Maria Pia, during her visit to Portugal in March 1905

Saturday afternoon, 1st February 1908, *Black Horse Square,* Lisbon Awaiting the return of the Royal Family from Vila Viçosa with members of the Government at the front of the quay side were (right to left) the Infante Dom Manuel, his uncle the Duke of Oporto and the dictator João Franco.

At 5 p.m. the ferry boat has arrived from the other side of the Tagus. The first to disembark was the Queen, Dona Amélia, followed by the King, Dom Carlos I. This was the last photograph taken of the King alive.

On the 31ˢᵗ January, whilst staying at the Ducal Palace at Vila Viçosa, where his ancestor had received the news of Portugal's independence and the consequent proclamation as the first King of the House of Braganza, Carlos signed a decree, drawn up by Franco, authorising the deportation of individuals denounced for threats to state security. Carlos is reputed to have foretold that: *I should not wonder if I were signing my own death warrant but it is no great matter*. There can be no doubt that regicide was planned, if not the complete annihilation of all the male members of the Royal Family, and the perpetrators hoped that a republic would spring up in the aftermath of the political confusion an assassination would cause. They had reckoned without the popularity of the King and the shock to public sentiment of their vile plot. There were those who believed Franco was the target but there were rumours circulating in Lisbon that the pig was going to be killed. This was a crude reference to the portly Carlos who had grown increasingly corpulent.

The Royal Family were due to return to Lisbon from Vila Viçosa on the afternoon of Saturday, 1ˢᵗ February 1908 and the morning papers had carried the news of the latest decree that the republican supporters considered illegal. Their expected arrival had been delayed by about an hour due to a train accident on the south side of the river Tagus. They were officially greeted by Government Ministers when they landed at the quay side, after crossing the Tagus, at *Black Horse Square*, in the late afternoon and the Queen was presented with a bouquet by a god-daughter. The accounts of what actually happened vary, including those of eye witnesses[8] but it was all over in minutes.

It was quite incredible that no proper precautions nor sensible safeguards had been organised to protect the Royal Family on their journey through the city . In fact there were only sixteen police on duty, instead of the usual forty, although the police commander, Colonel Correia, had asked for more. The King inquired from Franco about the general state of the capital and he who was so afraid on his own account that he slept at a different address each night, replied that all was peaceful and there was nothing to fear.

----

8 - Guilherme Pinto Basto was some forty yards behind the Royal Carriage at the time of the attack which he records as about 5 25 p.m. He was the cousin of the mother of Henry Stilwell, who kindly provided a copy of the account in English of the tragedy published first in *The Standard* on 18ᵗʰ February 1908 and then in the July 1908 edition of *The Lisbonian,* the students' magazine of the English College in Lisbon ; subsequently reprinted in the *'Twenty Fourth Annual Report & Review 1997'* of the British Historical Society of Portugal..

A contemporary photograph of *Black Horse Square* in 1908, taken from the north side, looking south towards the River Tagus, showing the west side of the square and the site of the assassinations. There are no photographs of the actual tragedy, as all the press photographers were at the quay side by the customs office, where the Royal Family disembarked. This is marked 5 and no longer exists. It is believed that the regicides met behind the kiosk marked 1, which also no longer stands. There were at least three assassins, possibly five. They must have waited for well over an hour because the arrival of the Royal Family had been delayed.The spot marked 2 is to where Costa ran out and with his revolver shot the King in the back of the neck, at point blank range, at about 5 25 p.m. as the carriage passed by slowly. The position marked 3 was where the assassin who got away was seen firing with outstretched arms at the Crown Prince. Buiça, who had hidden a rifle under his overcoat, ran across the road firing at the Crown Prince, was seized and struck down at the place marked 4.

When the first shot was fired at the spot marked x, the leading pair of horses of the carriage had begun slowly to turn the corner of the square marked 6, into the *Rua do Arsenal* where there is a police station, just out of sight of the square Clearly the dreadful plan had to be executed before the police on duty there were alerted.

The coachman drove as quickly as possible through the doorway into the *Arsenal* where there were medical facilities. The body of the dead King was put on this mattress on the floor of the First Aid Room.

Manuel, who had returned to Lisbon to attend to his studies for entry to the Navy, joined the family at the quay side and sat with his brother, facing their parents in the open Royal Carriage that was drawn by two pairs of horses, driven by a coachman, Bento Caparica and a postilion, Manuel Nunes. The carriage was not escorted, nor were there any attendants on the back and the King's orderly officer of the day, Captain Francisco Figueira, went off duty to catch a tram home as the coach started on its fatal journey. The assassins met probably behind a kiosk on the west side of the square, well away from the official welcoming party on the quay side where there were police on duty. They were also out of sight of the police station situated just round the far corner of the square. There was no crowd of people gathered in the square, probably because of the belated arrival and the assassins' nerves must have been on tenterhooks because of the delay. The Royal Carriage travelled very slowly along the west side of the square to give time for the attendants' carriage to catch up but this had not left the quay side when the far corner was reached and the leading pair of horse began to turn, even more slowly. The Royal Family were literally a sitting target, when one of the assassins shouted out, as the carriage passed by, *It's them!*

The first assassin, Costa[9] , a salesman, ran up to the back of the Royal Carriage and shot the King from behind with a pistol, through the nape of his neck, before the carriage turned the corner. The Crown Prince stood up, and drawing his revolver, fired at the facing assassin. Queen Amélia turned round and threw her bouquet at the villain to deflect his aim, which may well have saved Manuel. The second assassin, Buiça[10], a school teacher who had made his will earlier that day, appeared from the opposite direction with a shot gun which he had concealed beneath his overcoat, and then fired into the face of the Crown Prince. Henrique Valente, an unarmed young private soldier, threw himself over Buiça who managed to break free. On hearing the shots the Royal orderly officer ran up and cut down Buiça with his sword but Captain Figueira was badly wounded in the leg at the hip. A policeman then seized Buiça who bit his finger but was then shot down dead.

----

9 - Alfredo Luis da Costa (1885-1908) born Castro Verde, Beja, shop-assistant in Lisbon, insolvent editor

10- Manuel dos Reis da Silva Buiça (1876-1908) Former sergeant in the Cavalry, not only a good shot but on leaving the army he taught at secondary level with remarkable success ; widower ; he cultivated few relationships outside his everyday work ; militant activist of anarchist secret society linked to the republicans ; both Buiça and Costa were determined republicans spurred by the failure of the 28th January revolt.

Some thirty different drawings of the Regicide scenario were subsequently soon published and most bore little resemblance to the facts, according to eye witnesses; indeed some of the localities depicted are the fantasies of foreign artists who had never seen *Black Horse Square.* Some were reproduced as postcards and can be found still for sale in Lisbon street markets. Two of the more accurate representations of the tragedy are reproduced, together with a fantasia from a newspaper published in Canton, depicting an imaginary Chinese version of the situation.

One of the best examples of draughtsmanship was by F. De Haenen and was published in *"The Graphic"* as a double page centre spread in their issue of the 15th February 1908. It is reproduced here, showing the scene just after Costa fired the first shot that killed the King with the Queen, turning round to throw her bouquet into Costa's face. The carriage is about to turn the corner and Buiça has appeared in the far left hand side, taking aim with his rifle, that had been concealed under his overcoat. The King's aide-de-camp, Captain Figueira, is drawn on horseback, accompanying the Royal Carriage and about to cut down Costa, with a dramatic sabre thrust from the saddle, when in reality Figueira had gone off-duty and ran back on foot.

The regicides' bodies were taken to the Morgue: Manuel Buiça, a primary school teacher and twenty-four year old Alfredo Costa, a salesman; together with the twenty-one year old innocent bystander who was accidentally shot by the police, Joao Sabino da Costa, employee of a nearby jewellers.

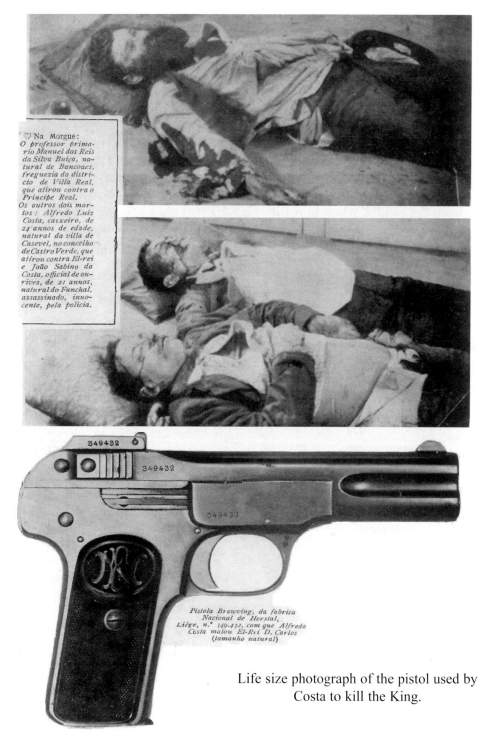

Na Morgue:
O professor primario Manuel dos Reis da Silva Buiça, natural de Bancoaes, freguezia do districto de Villa Real, que atirou contra o Principe Real.
Os outros dois mortos : Alfredo Luiz Costa, caixeiro, de 24 annos de edade, natural da villa de Casevel, no concelho de Castro Verde, que atirou contra El-rei e João Sabino da Costa, official de ourives, de 21 annos, natural do Funchal, assassinado, innocente, pela policia.

Pistola Browning, da fabrica Nacional de Herstal, Liége, n.º 349.432, com que Alfredo Costa matou El-Rei D. Carlos (tamanho natural)

Life size photograph of the pistol used by Costa to kill the King.

16

Photographs, reduced in size, of Buiça's cloak and rifle, with the pistol for comparison.
The postillion Costa wounded in his left hand ; the Royal carriage showing bullet holes in the door and the brave coachman Bento Caparica.

Carabina Winchester, modelo de 1907 n.º 2137, com que o professor Buiça matou o Principe Real D. Luiz Filippe

ASSASSINATION OF THE KING OF PORTUGAL AND THE CROWN PRINCE

(FROM A CORRESPONDENT.)

LISBON, Feb. 2

The terrible confusion and consternation which arose when the news of the assassination of the Sovereign and the Heir to the Throne was first spread abroad prevented the actual facts from becoming known. Now, however, the true details are being gradually ascertained, and they serve only to increase the horror of the deed.

A crowd had collected to see the Royal party drive from the banks of the Tagus to the Royal palace. The King and the rest of the Royal family entered the carriage in waiting, which advanced at the usual pace. Just as it was passing in front of the Ministry of Finance, a young fellow, almost a boy, dressed in what the Portuguese reporters call rough sporting attire, and with a revolver in his hand, rushed out from the midst of the throng of spectators and, running towards the carriage, jumped up behind. He at once fired at the King, who was wounded in the left side. Queen Amelia and the Crown Prince uttered cries of horror and dismay, and the Queen rose in the carriage and tried to strike a blow at the assassin with a bouquet which she was holding in her right hand. The fellow then fired a second shot, which hit the King in the back. His Majesty lifted his hand to his head and then fell back in a state of collapse on to his right side. All this passed in a moment, and then several people dashed forward and threw themselves upon the regicide who fell to the ground, firing, as he fell, a third shot, which struck no mark. Some one, probably a policeman, shot him dead as he lay on the ground.

BRAVERY OF THE QUEEN.

Meanwhile a tall man with black moustache and beard, who was wearing an enveloping mantle and had been standing by the Ministry of the Interior, drew forth a carbine which he had concealed under his cloak and moved forward towards the carriage. Taking aim full at the Crown Prince, he fired at him once and then again, the bullets taking effect in the face and the chest. He was about to fire a third shot when a policeman knocked up his arm, and the next moment the man was a corpse, falling under a rain of blows from the sword of a military officer . . . .

The scene at the Arsenal was heartbreaking. The Queen was beside herself with grief, horror, and shock, and uttered piteous cries as she turned her eyes from her dead husband to her dying son. The King and Prince were speedily but carefully carried out of the carriage into the medical hall of the Arsenal and there examined. Doctors came in haste and bent over the mattresses on which the victims had been laid. Blood was still gushing from the mouth and nose of the King. The doctors could only testify that he had breathed his last, death having been due to two wounds, one in the right infra-scapular region and the other in the vertebral column.

The Crown Prince when brought into the Arsenal was still living, but he survived only five minutes . . .

'The Times' printed this report, as the main news item of the day and repeated the text ninety years later, on 3rd February 1998, in the feature *'On this day'.*

After the Regicide, the new King, aged eighteen, with his wounded arm in a sling and his widowed mother, in mourning.

The cortège passing through *Black Horse Square* amid the tolling of the city bells and the booming of guns fired each minute in tribute.

Hence neither of these assassins survived the assassination but there was at least a third, seen firing at the Royal carriage and he got away; there may well have been others. The coachman had the presence of mind to drive fast round the corner into the shelter of Government buildings were there was a first-aid room. Other shots were fired by the police; one innocent bystander was killed and more were wounded, including the postilion. The King's brother, Afonso, had driven off for a motor ride as he was bored with waiting for the delayed arrival of the Royal Party. On hearing the shots of which there were some thirty to forty fired, he rushed back to *Black Horse Square* and knowing his dead brother's prowess, he put his hand into the King's right hand pocket and found lifeless fingers firmly clenched to a pistol, which Carlos had had no time left to draw. Nothing could save poor badly wounded Luís Filipe who may have shot the first assassin and then it took time for the Crown Prince[11] to die in agony. Manuel had been hit in the arm and sustained a nasty[12] wound but mercifully the Queen had been spared. The Royal survivors turned on Franco and the distraught Queen Mother Maria Pia reviled him with the words: *You promised to release the monarchy from its tomb and all that you have done has been to dig the graves of my son and grandson.*

Manuel II, who succeeded at eighteen, undeterred by the fact that his arm was in a sling, the next day issued a proclamation in which he promised to observe the Constitution and promptly dismissed Franco from office. The new Government abolished press censorship and many unconstitutional decrees, including the increase to the Civil List, which Manuel agreed was halved.

The shock of the regicide reverberated round the Royal Courts of a mainly monarchical Europe. Edward VII is said to have responded to the news almost with disbelief, retorting: *What! Two Knights of the Garter shot in the street in broad daylight!* The funeral was staged with great dignity, the cortège passing through *Black Horse Square*, past the scene of the shocking crime, without adverse demonstration or incident.

----

11 - The Guinness Book of Records used to list Luís Filipe as the shortest reigning monarch, but in fact he did not succeed to the throne as he was not proclaimed nor acclaimed sovereign. On the morning of that fatal day, his valet had loaded his pistol with six bullets, of which four were fired and two remained at the end of the tragedy. A cross scratched on the wall just inside the gateway to the Arsenal marks the spot where he expired.

12 - Passed off as a graze but his doctor's diary records a much more serious injury.

The paternal family tree of Dom Manuel II with the lineage of the Royal Houses of Braganza; Saxe-Coburg and Gotha, through his great-grandfather Fernando; Italy, through his paternal grand-mother Maria Pia; Austria, through her mother Adelhaide, daughter of Archduke Rainer of Austria.

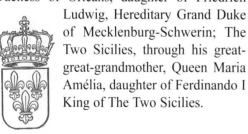

The maternal family tree of Dom Manuel II with the lineage of the Royal Houses of France, through his mother Queen Amélia; Spain, through his maternal grandmother, the Infanta Maria Isabel, Countess of Paris and her mother the Infanta Luisa Fernanda, Duchess of Montpensier; Mecklenburg, through his great-grandmother Hélène, Duchess of Orléans, daughter of Friedrich Ludwig, Hereditary Grand Duke of Mecklenburg-Schwerin; The Two Sicilies, through his great-great-grandmother, Queen Maria Amélia, daughter of Ferdinando I King of The Two Sicilies.

One of the first acts of King Manuel II's reign was his immediate termination of the ministry of João Franco. The dictator was seen to be crying like a child after being dismissed, leaving the Royal Palace with the former Minister of War, on 4th February 1908. Soon afterwards he left Portugal saying that the assassinations were a black page in history but he did not propose to be the historian.

The bearers of the swords and helmets of the
King and the Crown Prince: the Viscount
D'Asseca, Colonel Charters d'Azevedo, Dom
Fernando Serpa and the Marquess of Lavradio at
the top of the stairs outside St Vincent's awaiting
the coffins. Absolution was pronounced before
the procession entered the church.

The embalmed bodies of Dom Carlos I and the Crown Prince Dom Luís Filipe displayed in front of the High Altar of St. Vincent's. Their helmets and swords were placed at the foot of the coffins and in attendance were the Royal Guard of Archers with their halberds reversed.

The multitude outside St. Vincent's after the funeral when the public were admitted for several days to pay their respects.

Saturday, February 8th 1908 Requiem mass was said at St. James's Catholic Church, Spanish Place, London for the repose of the souls of the King and Crown Prince of Portugal. King Edward VII attended officially, escorted by his Household Cavalry and wearing the uniform of honorary colonel of the 3rd Portuguese Cavalry Regiment. Queen Alexandra wore ermine over her black silk dress and a mourning veil, likewise the British Princesses. Their Majesties were seated in the Sanctuary, with the Archbishop of Westminster in attendance. Mass was said by Bishop Brindle and the Portuguese Envoy, the Marques de Soveral was at the foot of the Sanctuary steps.

In the front row were the Prince and Princess of Wales (later King George V and Queen Mary), Prince and Princess Christian and Princess Louise, Duchess of Argyll (King Edward's brother - in-law and sisters). It is understood that this was the first time that officially a British Sovereign had attended Mass in a Roman Catholic Church since the Reformation i.e. for over three centuries. This caused protests from Protestant extremists in spite of the Anglo-Portuguese Alliance and the fact that Dom Carlos had attended the funeral of Queen Victoria.

MOURNING FOR KING CARLOS: THE KING AND QUEEN LEAVING ST. PAUL'S AFTER THE SPECIAL SERVICE.

GRAPHIC, FEBRUARY 15, 1908

The King and Queen, accompanied by Princess Victoria, were present last Sunday at the special memorial service in St. Paul's Cathedral for the late King and Crown Prince of Portugal. The Royal visit was of a private nature, and there was no escort or guard of honour, their Majesties driving to the Cathedral in a private carriage. The impressive service was attended by a large congregation, who remained seated until the King and Queen-preceded by the Lord Mayor, with his Sword and Mace bearers-had left the church..

Prayers for dead princes

The Church Times.
February 15th, 1908.

ON SUNDAY, "being the day after the burial of his late Majesty Charles, King of Portugal and the Algarves, Duke of Saxony, K.G., and his Royal Highness Louis Philippe, Crown Prince of Portugal, Duke of Braganza, K.G.," their Majesties the King and Queen, together with the members of the Royal Family, attended an obituary service at St Paul's. The Bishop of London was out of the country at the time, but the Primate was present. A great impression was produced by the beautiful "Russian Kontakion for the departed", which ought to be better known than it is. . . Having said this, we feel at liberty to express regret that the commemoration of the departed Princes was

not made at a Solemn Eucharist. A great opportunity was missed for showing that the Church of England, in common with the whole Catholic Church, associates with the Eucharistic offering the dead no less than the living. It would then not have been possible for the newspapers to contrast with the Mass offered in St James's, Spanish-place, the improvised sort of function at St Paul's, which seemed, in its petitions, to have far more reference to ourselves than to those for whose souls presumably we were praying. In that case, too, there would have been less justification for the King's appearance in the Spanish Church, and we should have been spared the astonishing statement in a Church contemporary that "on Saturday a King of England attended Mass in his own dominions for the first time since the abdication of James II."

THE TIMES - 1 February 2008

COURT

In memorium -

KING CHARLES OF PORTUGAL AND HIS SON PRINCE LUÍS FILIPE In homage to the Portuguese community in London, the Monarch, the Head of the Armed Forces, the Patriot and the Man of His Time, a Mass will be held today at 6pm, in His memory and that of His Son, assassinated on February 1st 1908, at "Farm Street Jesuit Church of the Immaculate Conception", 114 Mount Street, Mayfair, London W1K 3AH

His Royal Highness the Duke of Braganza unveiling on 1st February 2006 a plaque erected in *Black Horse Square* on the site of the Regicide. The words on the plaque read:-

AT THIS PLACE
ON 1st FEBRUARY 1908
H.M. THE KING DOM CARLOS I
AND THE CROWN PRINCE
DOM LUÍS FILIPE
DIED FOR THEIR COUNTRY

Father and son were sincerely mourned by the stunned Portuguese people and amongst those in tears at St Vincent's was the old lighthouse keeper from Cascais, who had saved Carlos from drowning thirty-five years before. To this day solemn Requiem Mass for the repose of their souls is said at St Vincent's every year on 1st February in sad memory of their murder; Thousands attended on the centenary in 2008

The apt presence of the King and Queen Alexandra at the memorial Requiem Mass at St James's Church, Spanish Place, London marked the first occasion of a post-Reformation British Sovereign's attendance at a Roman Catholic service but led to adverse comment from some bigoted Protestants. Edward VII retorted that Dom Carlos had attended his mother's viz Queen Victoria's funeral The King also attended a memorial service at St Paul's cathedral.

In more recent times a statue of a poignant female, cloaked in medieval fashion and with her hands hiding her face in shame, was placed by their tombs The figure represents Portugal mourning over the bodies of her dead King Carlos *The Martyred* and his heir, Luís Filipe, for their undeserved horrendous deaths. This beautiful memorial, entitled *Grief = O Dor* is the exquisite work of the famous Portuguese sculptor Francisco Franco, who also executed the impressive statue of *Christ the King* that dominates the River Tagus. On 1st February 2006 His Royal Highness the Duke of Braganza unveiled a memorial plaque at the place of the Regicide. The President attended the centenary ceremony of the erection of a new statue of the sailor King in Cascais on 1st February 2008.

On the plinth of the statue of Carlos that stands outside the Ajuda Palace is recorded the tribute of the Portuguese to the achievements of his reign:-
He consolidated the Portuguese overseas territories; re-organised the army and the navy; defended the nation's greatness by self-sacrifice. He cultivated and protected the arts and sciences; promoted agriculture and public works. He restored our prestige in Europe; began financial reforms and raised money values.

Manuel II - *The Unfortunate:*

Manuel II was heartily acclaimed as the new young King but, as an intelligent, well educated man, he probably realised that the dynasty was doomed, particularly as he had just missed being assassinated himself. Some three months after the regicide, King Manuel II wrote down on 21st May his account of the tragedy, in twenty-two numbered pages of his handwriting, headed *'Absolutely intimate notes'*. He entitled the cover *'My Memories after 1st February 1908'* together with his signature *D. Manuel Rei* and here follow his own poignant words:

King Manuel II opening the first parliament of his reign on 29th April 1908.

The Marquess of Lavradio, the King's private secretary.

*O marquês do Lavradio
Secretário parlicular d' El-Rei
D. Manuel*

'Ever since a few days after 1st February, the day of the horrific attack when I lost my beloved father and such a dear brother, both barbarously assassinated, I have had the idea of writing for myself these intimate notes. What I am writing here is just as it comes but I am frankly and clearly going to recount without elegance everything that happened. If God gives me health and strength, perhaps one day this could be of interest for me. This is a declaration that I make to myself. Since this is an intimate story of my reign I am going to begin with the horrific and cruel outrage.

On 1st February Their Majesties the King Dom Carlos I, the Queen Senhora Dona Amélia and His Highness the Crown Prince [13] were returning from Vila Viçosa where I might have still have been. I had come earlier (some days before) for reason of preparing my studies for the Naval School. I had stayed two days at Vila Viçosa then had returned to Lisbon. In the capital everything was in a state of extraordinary agitation as well it might be as here on the 28th January a revolution was attempted which did not succeed. Many people were implicated in this attempt: it was after that night of the 28th that the Minister of Justice Teixeira de Abreu[14] took to Vila Viçosa the famous decree which was published on the 31st January. It was a sad coincidence that it had been published on the day of the anniversary of the Revolt of Oporto.

My Father did not have any desire to return to Lisbon. I remember well that I was returning to Lisbon a fortnight before and that my Father wanted to stay at Vila Viçosa : my Mother on the contrary forcibly wanted to come. I recollect perfectly this phrase which he said to me on the day, or the day before, I came back to Lisbon after spending two days in Vila Viçosa: *If I could only break a leg and not go back to Lisbon on 1st February!*

It would have been better if they had not returned because then I would not have lost two people so dear to me and today I would not find myself King! However, Thy Will be done, O Lord!

----

13 - Dom Manuel refers to his parents and brother by their formal styles. 'The Crown Prince' in Portuguese is literally 'the Prince Royal' with the style of Highness rather than Royal Highness which would be tautological. The dignity of *Most Faithful Majesty=Magestade fidelíssima* was conferred on King John V of Portugal by Pope Benedict XIV in 1748.

14 - Teixeira de Abreu had been appointed Minister of Justice on 2 May 1907.

António José de Almeida (1866-1929) President of the Portuguese Republic 1919-23

João Pinto dos Santos (1856-1946) Lawyer and liberal politician of the extreme left

Afonso Costa (1871-1937) lawyer; republican deputy 1900, leader of the Democratic Republican Party, 1st Minister of Justice, Head of Government and Minister of Finance 1913-14 & 1915-16

Manuel dos Reis da Silva Buiça (1876-1908) militant activist of anarchist secret society linked to the republicans

Caricatura de José M. de Alpoim, por Leal da Câmara.

José Maria de Alpoim (1858-1916) collaborated with the abortive republican revolt on 28 January, he was exiled , returned on the implementation of the Republic, fluent orator and journalist.

Alfredo Luis da Costa (1885-1908) shop-assistant in Lisbon, insolvent editor

30

But to return to the said decree of the 31ˢᵗ January; Already various important politicians had been arrested : António José de Almeida,[15] republican and former deputy, João Chagas[16], republican, João Pinto dos Santos,[17] dissident and former deputy; the Viscount da Ribeira Brava[18] and others. This António José de Almeida is one of the most genuine republicans and really believes in it, so they say. João Pinto dos Santos is also one of the most genuine of his party; the Viscount da Ribeira Brava is pretty useless and had been arrested with arms in his hands on 28ᵗʰ January. However António José de Almeida and J. Pinto dos Santos could not be tried except by the Chamber of Deputies, as they had been deputies in the last Chamber. Well, I believe that the intention of the Government was to send some of them to Timor, thus removing by a dictatorial decree one of the most important rights of the deputies. Counsellor José Maria de Alpoim[19], Peer of the Realm, and head of the dissident party, had had his house surrounded by police but afterwards had fled to Spain. Another dissident as well had fled to Spain and went about there disguised.

----

15 -   António José de Almeida (1866-1929) Medical doctor ; President of the Portuguese Republic 1919-23 , until 1926 he was the only President who completed his term of office.

16 -   João Pinheiro Chagas (1863-1925) Journalist ; violently denounced the Monarchy, head of the first Republican Government 1911 , ambassador in Paris.

17 -   João Pinto dos Santos (1856-1946) Lawyer and liberal politician of the extreme left ; graduated Coimbra 1882 having studied Law and Theology, supported the students in an academic strike, notable fencer and athlete specialising in gymnastics and weight lifting, elected to parliament 1887 as a deputy of the Progressive Party, successively re-elected until 1909, after the implementation of the Republic remained a deputy by length of service for many years, civil governor of Santarém, legal adviser of the Ministry of Colonies, his library had an important collection of works on Jurisprudence and Philosophy.

18 -   Francisco Correa de Herédia (1852-1918); born Ribeira Brava, Madeira, Civil Governor of Braganza, Beja & Lisbon, deputy for Madeira 1897-99, created 1st and only Viscount da Ribeira Brava 1871 ; former Monarchist turned republican and known by his title without the honour of Viscount ;   his family strongly disapproved and his son warned the King of the impending danger ; provided munitions for the revolution ; led the republicans as they paraded through Lisbon on 4 October 1910 ; assassinated 1918 by disaffected republicans. He was the great-great-grandfather of Her Royal Highness, the Duchess of Braganza, Dona Isabel de Herédia.

19 -   José Maria de Alpoim (1858-1916) graduated in Law Coimbra University, joined the Progressive Party 1878, worked in the Exchequer, Minister of Justice 1889, 1904 & 1905, his negative and disintegrative attitude to the political monarchist forces contributed greatly to the fall of the Monarchy, having collaborated with the abortive republican revolt on 28 January, he was exiled, returned on the implementation of the Republic, fluent orator and journalist.

Dom Manuel's timetable of studies before his accession

The following timetable of studies was drawn up primarily to prepare Dom Manuel for entry to the Navy by competitive examinations and is taken from 'Dom Manuel II -História do Seu Reinado' by Rocha Martins.

Daily routine : Rise at 6 a.m. ; preparations for studies 7am - 8 30 am ;
lessons 9 am - 1145 am ; lunch and recreation 11 45 am - 1 45 pm ;
lessons 1 45pm -3 pm ; exercise 3 pm - 5 30 pm ; lessons 5 30 pm - 7pm ;
dinner 7pm - 8pm ; Music/practise 8pm -10pm

	Mondays	Tuesdays	Wednesdays	Thursdays	Fridays	Saturdays
9 -10	Gymnastics & Fencing	General Science & natural history	English	German & History	Gymnastics & Fencing	Mathematics
10-11 45	German , History & Geography	Mathematics	Portuguese literature	Mathematics	History	English
1 45 - 3	Drawing	Physics & Chemistry	Portuguese history	Portuguese	Physics & Chemistry	History of Portuguese literature
3 - 5 30 *	Walking & Riding	Walking & Riding	Riding lesson	Walking & Riding	Walking & Riding	Walking & Riding
5 30 - 7	French	Mathematics	Mathematics	Mathematics	French	Mathematics
8 - 10			Music lesson			Piano lesson

* n. b. Apart from Fencing, the absence of any competitive sport or team participation, yet Dom Manuel later became an adept and keen lawn tennis player. Were his Saturdays' lessons on the history of Portuguese literature, the inspiration that led to his becoming a great bibliophile ? By any standards, this academic regime must have been tough for a normal teenager. Nevertheless, it would have served him in good stead when he so abruptly became King. Below are photographs of his teachers taken from *'Illustração Portugueza'* - no 144 - 23 November 1908 :-

Prof Alfredo King
English

Padre Domingos Fiadeiro
Portuguese

Prof Boeyé
French

Prof Marques Leitão
Mathematics

Prof Achilles Machado
Natural Sciences

Prof Fontoura da Costa
Mathematics

Prof Rey Colaço
Music

Another one arrested was Afonso Costa[20]: he is of the worst that exists not only in Portugal but in all the World; he is fearful and cowardly, but intelligent and will stoop to anything to achieve his aims.

Well all this is merely a prelude before I begin in more detail the intimate story of my reign.

As I said before I was in Lisbon on the 28th January; a friend of mine (who if I am not mistaken was my teacher Abel Fontoura da Costa)[21] told one of the ministers that I would like to know something about what was going on, because there was such commotion. João Franco then wrote me a letter that I greatly regret tearing up, because in that letter he told me that everything was quiet and there was nothing to fear. What blind stupidity! However let us go on to the fatal day of Saturday 1st February In the morning I had had coaching from Marques Leitão[22] and King[23] . I calmly had lunch with the Viscount Asseca[24] and Kerausch[25]. After lunch I was playing the piano, very pleased, because on that day *Tristan and Isolde* by Wagner was going to be performed for the first time at São Carlos.[26]

----

20 - Afonso Costa (1871-1937) lawyer ; republican deputy 1900, made a great impact on public opinion in the campaign to destroy the Monarchy, leader of the Democratic Republican Party, 1st Minister of Justice, immediately introduced the legislation to ban religious orders followed by the law separating the Church and the State ; Head of Government and Minister of Finance 1913-14 & 1915-16 , promoted the intervention of Portugal in the 1st World War 1914-18, exiled to France 1918 during the dictatorship of Sidónio Pais; 1919 president of the Portuguese delegation at the Peace Conference ; until 1926 leader of Portugal's delegation to the League of Nations then replaced by the Military Regime.

21 - Abel Fontoura da Costa (1869-1940) Historian & Politician, Naval officer, teacher Naval Academy, director 1936-39 ; Governor Cape Verde 1915-17 ; Minister of Agriculture & the Navy 1923 ; author of works on navigation and the discoveries; taught Dom Manuel mathematics. The prince was well educated and a diligent student ; his neatly written exercise books can still be seen at Vila Viçosa

22 - Carlos Adolfo Marques Leitão, Colonel, director of the Marquess de Pombal school, taught Dom Manuel arithmetic and geometry from 1903.

23 - Alfredo King, Dom Manuel's English teacher since April 1903; teacher at the Industrial Institute

24 - Dom Salvador Correa de Sá e Benevides (1873-1939) 9th Viscount de Asseca ; 11th *almotacé-mór,* bore the train of Dom Manuel's mantle at his acclamation ceremony and handed the sceptre to the enthroned King ; at Mafra when the Royal Family left on 5 October 1910; inherited a fortune from his diplomat uncle, the Marquess de Soveral,who died childless in Paris 1922; Dom Manuel's executor; accompanied the King's body back to Lisbon 1932.

25 - Dr Franz Kerausch, Austrian; personal tutor of the Crown Prince since 1899.

26 - In the event the performance was cancelled.

The evening before I had been playing a 4-hand version of Beethoven's Septet with my dear Master Alexandre Rey Colaço[27] which was and is one of the works I like best of this musical genius. After lunch at the usual time, that is to say at quarter to two I began my lesson with Fontoura da Costa because he had changed the time of his lesson with Padre Fiadeiro[28] . Fontoura's time was at half past five.

I finished with Fontoura at three o'clock, and a little later received a telegram from my beloved mother, saying there had been a derailment at Casa Branca, nothing serious, but they would be three quarters of an hour late. I thanked God that nothing had happened, but, as can be imagined, I had no idea of what was going to happen; now I wonder; did that derailment just happen by chance? Or was it planned to delay their arrival? I do not know. Now I am doubtful; after the horror of what happened, many things remain in doubt.

A little after four o'clock, I left the Necessidades Palace[29] in a landau with the Viscount de Asseca, to meet Their Majesties and His Highness at the Terreiro do Paço[30]. We went via Pampulha, Janelas Verdes, Aterro and Rua do Arsenal. We arrived at the Terreiro do Paço. At the ferry station there were a lot of people from the Court, and others. I spoke first with the Minister of War, Vasconcelos Porto[31], perhaps the minister I liked best in João Franco's government. He said that everything was all right. We had quite a long wait; finally the boat carrying my parents and brother arrived. I embraced them, we moved to the entrance and the four of us got into the carriage. My mother sat in the back, with my poor father on her left; my dear brother sat in front of my father, and I in front of my mother.

----

27 -   Alexandre Rey Colaço (1854-1928), pianist and composer, music teacher at the Conservatory in Lisbon ; Dom Manuel was musically gifted and could play well both the piano and organ.

28 - Padre João Damasceno (Domingos) Fiadeiro, former teacher at the seminary of Santarém, teacher of Portuguese literature to the Crown Prince 1902-5, then taught Dom Manuel.

29 - Necessidades Palace- the principal residence of the Royal Family when in Lisbon ; nowadays the Portuguese Foreign Office.

30 - Terreiro do Paço called *Black Horse Square* by the British after the equestrian statue of King José in the centre, reigned 1750-77 ; the statue commemorates the re-building of Lisbon after the 1755 earthquake and the horse was modelled on his favourite thoroughbred bay *Gentil* of the famous Lusitanian classic *Alter Real* stud created by the King.

31 - António Carlos Coelho de Vasconcelos Porto; Minister of War 19 May 1906- 4 February 1908

What I am going to write now is the most difficult of all for me: when I think of those horrible moments I went through, my impressions get confused. What a dreadful evening and night! Nobody in this world can have an idea or even imagine what it was like! I believe that only my poor, beloved mother and I really know.

I am now going to describe what happened in that historic square. We left the station quite slowly. As my mother was telling me about how the derailment at Casa Branca had happened, the first shot was heard in the middle of the square; I did not hear it, but it must have been the signal: the signal to begin that monstrous outrage, for it could be said, and I do say, that it was the signal to start the hunt. It was exactly what you do when hunting down wild beasts: you find out where they will pass, and when they do, a signal is given and the firing starts! Villains!

I was looking towards the statue of King José I and I saw a man with a black beard, wearing a great cloak. I saw this man open the cloak and take out a carbine. So far was I from imagining the horror of what was to happen, that I said to myself, knowing how edgy the whole situation was, "what a stupid joke!" The man left the pavement and came up behind the carriage and opened fire.

Here I shall make a little sketch to help me.
1.   Statue of King José
2.   Position of Buiça, the man with the beard
3.   Where he opened fire
4.   Approximate position of the carriage when he opened fire
5.   Gateway of the Arsenal
6.   Pelourinho Square
7.   Approximately where that Costa, who killed my father, came from

When I saw the fearsome-looking bearded man aim at the carriage, I realised what was happening. My God, the horror! Only God, I and my mother know what happened then; because even my beloved and dearly missed brother had only a few seconds before he too was mown down.

My God, how I miss them! Give me strength, O Lord to bear this very heavy cross to Calvary! Only You, my God, know how I have suffered!

1. Statue of King José
2. Position of Buiça, the man with the beard
3. Where he opened fire
4. Approximate position of the carriage when he opened fire
5. Gateway of the Arsenal
6. Pelourinho Square
7. Approximately where that Costa, who killed my father, came from

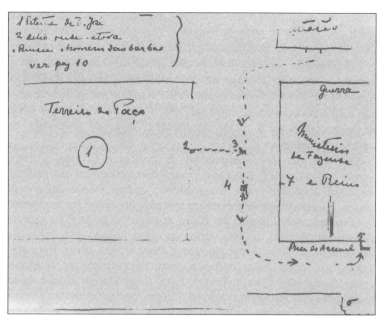

Dom Salvador Correa de Sá e Benevides (1873-1939)
9th Viscount de Asseca;
Dom Manuel's executor

Canon Aires Pacheco

36

Immediately after Buiça had opened fire (I do not know if he hit anyone), rapid gunfire broke out as if wild beasts were being hunted down!

No security measures had been taken in the Terreiro do Paço! That is what I find so hard to forgive João Franco. If he made mistakes during his government, especially in the period of the dictatorship, that is less important for me. I am sure his intentions were very good; it was the means that were bad, appalling, for the result was more atrocious than anyone might imagine. When people told him that things were bad and that there were anarchists in our country, he did not believe them.

The first symptom that I remember was the explosion of those bombs in Rua de Santo António in Estrela. I well remember the impression it made on me when I first heard! It was summer and we were at Pena, Sintra. Who could have said what would happen six or eight months later! But to return to the terrifying attack.

I know that one of the police commanders, Colonel Correia, was very worried and that João Franco did not believe that anything unpleasant could happen, least of all such a horror as this, and unfortunately no precautionary measures at all were taken.

Immediately after Buiça opened fire, another man came out of the arcade of the Ministries and shot my father several times at point-blank range; one of the bullets entered his back, and another the back of his head, which killed him immediately. What villains! As if their atrocious malice and frightful cowardice were not enough, they shot him from behind.

After this, I hardly remember what happened, it was all so quick. I do clearly remember my beloved, heroic mother standing up in the carriage, with a bunch of flowers in her hand, shouting at those damned animals, because people they were not, *Villains! You villains!*

There was enormous confusion. I also remember, and this I shall never forget, as we turned from the Terreiro de Paço into Rua do Arsenal, I saw my brother standing up in the carriage, pistol in hand. I can say of him only what Canon Aires Pacheco said at the obsequies in the Jerónimos: *He died a hero, at the side of his King*! For me that is what best expresses what I feel.

My God, what horror! When I think of this tremendous disaster it still seems to be a nightmare!

ICONOGRAPHIA DO ATTENTADO

O attentado de 1 de fevereiro

RECONSTITUIÇÃO DE CHARLES M. SHELDON, NO «BLACK & WHITE» DE 6 DE FEVEREIRO

When I glanced at my brother, already in Rua do Arsenal, I saw that he had fallen to the right, with an enormous wound on the left side of his face, blood gushing from it like a fountain! I took out a handkerchief and tried to staunch the flow: but what could I do? The handkerchief was immediately sodden.

Amidst all this tremendous confusion, we did not know where the carriage should go: we thought of the Estrela hospital, but then decided the Arsenal would be better.

In the Rua do Arsenal, I too had been hit in the arm. I felt a blow, something like a whiplash: it was in my upper right arm. Now I think back to that frightening day, and the terrible event, I feel, and am almost certain (I do not want to be more definite because at moments of anguish like this, you lose your sense of things) that I escaped because I had instinctively moved to the left.

In the second carriage came the Count and Countess de Figueiró[32] and the Marquess de Alvito[33], and in the third Viscount de Asseca, Vice-Admiral Guilherme A. Brito de Capelo[34] and Major António Waddington[35] As we drove through the gateway of the Arsenal, the Countess de Figueiró got into our carriage, and I remember Viscount de Asseca and Count de Figueiró at the side of the carriage. Once in the Arsenal, I got out of the carriage, followed by my dear Mother.

Our escape was a real miracle: God wished to spare us! I thank God for leaving me the mother that I love so much. She has always been the person I have most loved in this world and every day I thank God for saving her for me! When my beloved mother got out of the carriage she went straight up to João Franco, who was already there, and said, or rather shouted, in a voice that invoked fear, *They have killed The King: they have killed my son!* She seemed to have gone mad. And no wonder: I do not know how I myself did not go mad.

----

32 - Dom António de Vasconcelos e Sousa (1858-1922) ; 2nd Count de Figueiró, chamberlain of Queen Amélia, diplomat, minister plenipotentiary in Rome, went into exile with the King on 5 October 1910; died in England. The Countess was a lady in waiting of Queen Amélia.

33 - Dom José Lobo da Silveira Quaresma (1826-1917); 4th Marquess de Alvito, 16th Baron de Alvito. Peer of the Realm, High Official of the Royal Household; from the stock of the first Barons of the Realm, carried the Crown at the acclamation ceremony of Dom Manuel.

34 - Guilherme Augusto Brito de Capelo (1839-1926); Vice-Admiral and scientist, served in the Navy 1853-1908, 1870 first European to descend the crater of the highest peak on the Isle of Fogo, Cape Verde; honorary aide-de-camp of Dom Luís and Dom Carlos.

35 Major António Waddington; orderly officer accompanied Dom Manuel from Mafra to Ericeira 5 October 1910

The entrance to the Arsenal : visitors looking at the spot where the Crown Prince died marked by a cross scratched on the wall

Portuguese dignatories at Dom Manuel's wedding 1913:front row: srs. marquez de Faial, condes de Sabugosa e Tarouca, second row: srs. marquez de Lavradio, secretário de D. Manuel, Salvador Asseca, Camelo Lampreia, antigo ministro de Portugal no Brazil, Dr D. António de Lencastre, antigo medico

Countess de Figueiró

What happened then in those hours in the Arsenal no one can imagine. The first thing was that I lost all sense of time. I grasped the arm of my poor and beloved mother and would not let go, asking Countess de Figueiró not to leave her. Meanwhile, many people from the Court, diplomats, ministers and even honorary ministers of State, were coming in. We were still in doubt (which unfortunately did not last long) whether the two people we loved so much were still alive! There were many doctors there, among others Dr Bossa (who I think was the first to arrive), Dr Moreira Júnior[36] and Dr António Lencastre.

Later, (some days later) Dr Bossa told me that as soon as he arrived he had struck a match and the pupils of my brother's eyes had contracted. But when he repeated the experiment, not even this little sign of life remained.

May you rest in eternal peace, and may God guard your soul!

I had no hope that my father, or even my brother, would survive. With such terrible wounds it seemed impossible.

As I have said, all the government were there except for the Minister of the Exchequer, Martins de Carvalho[37]. What I shall never be able to forget is that although he was a member of the government of my poor father when he was assassinated, he did not go to the Arsenal! It is said (though I am not stating this as fact) that he fled up to the attic of the Ministry of Finance and locked himself in! Whatever, it is now six months since my dear father and brother were assassinated and he has never appeared here! I think that this is absolutely extraordinary - to say the least!

My poor grandmother[38] at the Ajuda Palace was asked to come to the Arsenal. I was not present when she arrived. My arm was being treated in the office of the Inspector of the Arsenal.

----

36 - Manuel António Moreira Júnior (1888-1953); doctor and politician, graduate of Lisbon Medical School, thesis on Tuberculosis, chair of Pathology ; Deputy Progressive Party 1897, Minister for the Navy and Overseas 1905-06, Minister for Public Works 1909, president of the Academy of Sciences and Society of Geography of Lisbon.

37 - Fernando Augusto Miranda Martins de Carvalho (1872-1947); Minister of the Exchequer 2 May 1907- 4 February 1908 ; diplomat & essayist ; graduated in law Coimbra, lawyer in Oporto, deputy 1901, emigrated to Brazil on proclamation of the Republic.

38 - Princess Maria Pia of Savoy (1847-1911), daughter of King Victor Emanuel II who unified Italy ; 1862 married Dom Luís who reigned 1861-89 ; the Ajuda Palace was their main Lisbon residence. When criticised for extravagance she retorted *Those that want Queens should pay !* Her brother King Umberto I of Italy had been shot dead at close range at Monza in 1900.

After luncheon in the Portuguese Legation in London, Dom Manuel with the Marquess of Lavradio, the Count of Sabugosa and the Marquess of Faial

Queen Amélia at the cathedral in Lisbon, photographed before entering with on the right, Dom José de Avilez Lobo de Almeida Melo de Castro (1872-1972); 9th Count de Galveias, chamberlain of Queen Amélia

and on leaving with on the left António Maria José de Melo Silva César e Meneses (1854-1923); 9th Count de Sabugosa; last High Steward of the Royal Household

When my grandmother arrived she went straight up to my mother and said[39], *They have killed my son!* and my mother replied, *And mine, too!* May God give me strength.

But before this there are various things I want to recount. My poor, beloved mother was walking to and fro in the Arsenal with different people - the Count de Sabugosa[40], the Count and Countess de Figueiró, the Count and Countess de Galveias[41] and others - always talking in a state of agitation that I cannot describe but is easy to understand.

Suddenly she collapsed onto the ground! Only God and I know how frightened I was! After what had happened there came this reaction and I do not even want to say what passed through my mind! Then I realised what it was: the terrible shock was having its effect! My mother got up, almost ashamed at having fallen. She is truly heroic. If only many men had a tenth of my mother's courage. She has been a real martyr! What I pray to God always and at every instant is to protect her for my sake!

Shortly after we arrived at the Arsenal, Major Waddington came to say that our dear ones were still alive; but unfortunately he soon came back, in tears. *Well?* I asked him. He made no reply. I told him I was strong enough to hear everything. Then he told me that they were both dead! Grant them, Lord, eternal rest and may Your eternal Light shine upon them, Amen!

----

39 - Dom Manuel recorded that both Queens spoke to each other in French viz *On a tué mon fils. Et le mien aussi.* It is also said that the Queen Mother reviled Franco with the words *You promised to release the Monarchy from its tomb and all that you have done has been to dig the graves of my son and grandson.*

40 - António Maria José de Melo Silva César e Meneses (1854-1923); 9th Count de Sabugosa; diplomat, graduated in Law from Coimbra; 1880 elected to Parliament as a deputy of the Progressive Party; succeeded his father in 1897 as a Peer of the Realm;1903 last High Steward of the Royal Household ; Grand Cross of the Orders of Christ and Santiago ; accompanied the King on 5 October 1910 and visited the Royal Family in exile ; 1919 imprisoned for a few weeks during the short lived Restoration of the Monarchy in the North ; published a variety of stories, poetry and plays ; 1887-94 one of the celebrated group called *Life's defeated/ os Vencidos da Vida dilettantes;* on the first anniversary of his death in 1924, Dom Manuel wrote a fine tribute, in memory of his loyal friend.

41 - Dom José de Avilez Lobo de Almeida Melo de Castro (1872-1972); 9th Count de Galveias, Peer of the Realm, High Official of the Royal Household, Chief Ranger of the Royal enclosures and of the Royal game park of Vila Viçosa, chamberlain of Queen Amélia; married 1894 Dona Teresa de Lancastre e Oliveira 1870-1939, daughter of the Viscount de Barcelinhos.

Dr Thomas de Mello
Breyner (1866-1933) ;
4th Count de Mafra;
doctor of the Royal
Household

Aires de Ornelas e Vasconcelos
(1866-1930); Minister for the
Navy and Overseas 1906-08, after
the fall of the Monarchy 1910,
Dom Manuel appointed him his
surrogate-lieutenant in Portugal

Countess de Sabugosa Dona
Mariana das Dores de Mello
(1856-1952);
lady in waiting of Queen Dona
Maria Pia and Queen Dona
Amélia

Dona Helena Maria de Sales de Borja de Assis de Paula de Sousa Holstein de Sampaio e Pina
de Brederode, (1864-1941) only surviving child of the 3rd Duchess of Palmela; created 3rd
Marquesa de Faial 1881, carried the bride's train at Dom Manuel's wedding 4th September 1913
at Sigmaringen and on that day created 4th Duchess of Palmela by the King.

A little later, I saw João Franco with Aires de Ornelas[42] (Minister for the Navy) and perhaps (I cannot be sure of this) Vasconcelos Porto, Minister of War, going to the Sala da Balança to telephone for all necessary measures to be taken. These are scenes that should I live a hundred years will remain engraved on my heart. Now it was night, which made everything even more horrifying and sinister: by then, there were many people in the Arsenal, and we started thinking of our return to the Necessidades Palace. As I write these lines now, I am reliving all this with horror! Then we got into a closed landau, my grandmother, my mother, the Count de Sabugosa and myself. We left the Arsenal by the Cais de Sodré gate, where there was a squadron of the Municipal guard under the command of Lieutenant Paul. Colonel Alfredo de Albuquerque rode on the box; as we left the Count de Sabugosa was given a revolver; my grandmother also wanted one. We then rode at full speed back to the Necessidades Palace. Waiting to meet us at the entrance were the Duchess of Palmela[43], Marquesa de Faial[44] ,Countess de Sabugosa[45], Dr Thomas de Mello Breyner[46], the Count Tattenbach, German Envoy, and his Countess, and many of the household servants. It was a horrible scene, with everyone in tears. We went very slowly upstairs amidst the weeping and sobbing of everybody present. I accompanied my poor, beloved mother to her room, and left my poor grandmother in the drawing room.'

----

42 - Aires de Ornelas e Vasconcelos (1866-1930); Minister for the Navy and Overseas 19 May 1906-4 February 1908; enlisted in the cavalry, Mozambique 1895, head of general staff of Mouzinho de Alburquerque, decorated with the Order of the Tower and Sword, returned to Portugal 1898; after the fall of the Monarchy 1910, Dom Manuel appointed him his surrogate-lieutenant in Portugal; led the Monarchist uprising at Monsanto outside Lisbon on 22 January 1919.

43 - Dona Maria Luiza Domingues de Sales de Borja de Assis de Paula de Sousa Holstein b 1841; 3rd Duchess of Palmela, eldest daughter of 2nd Duke of Palmela who did not have sons, Dame of the Order of St Isabel, Lady in waiting of Queen Maria Pia.

44 - Dona Helena Maria de Sales de Borja de Assis de Paula de Sousa Holstein de Sampaio e Pina de Brederode (1864-1941) only surviving child of the 3rd Duchess of Palmela; cr 3rd Marquesa de Faial 1881, accompanied the Royal Family 5 October 1910, carried the bride's train at Dom Manuel's wedding 4 September 1913 at Sigmaringen and on that day created 4th Duchess of Palmela by the King.

45 - Countess de Sabugosa Dona Mariana das Dores de Mello (1856-1952); 4th Countess of Murça, married the 9th Count de Sabugosa 1876 ; lady in waiting of Queen Dona Maria Pia and Queen Dona Amélia; accompanied the Royal Family 5 October 1910.

46 - Dr Thomas de Mello Breyner (1866-1933) ; 4th Count de Mafra; graduated from the Lisbon Medical School, dermatologist , 1891 doctor of the Royal Household, director of the clinical service in the Civil Hospitals of Lisbon, his diaries for 1908-13 have been published. On Saturday 1st February 1908 he records that he greeted the King and Crown Prince after they landed and then left the Square. On hearing the terrible news he returned to see the coaches leaving with the dead and then he went to the Palace, where he stayed all night. On Tuesday 2 March he visited the wounded Francisco Figueira.

The attic in the *Mouraria,* marked above on the photograph by two white + signs where the widower Buiça lived with his two children, Elvira, seven years old and Manuel aged five months. Funds were raised by Republicans for their adoption

The graves of the assassins became shrines for Republican sympathisers

Little seems to have been done to bring to justice those responsible for plotting the crime[47] and the graves of the two dead assassins became shrines for republican sympathisers, who competed with each other to provide for the orphans left bereft by Buiça. It seems incredible that the brave orderly officer, who did his duty in striking down that assassin and was badly wounded himself, had to leave the country to avoid retaliation, as the republicans clamoured that he should be charged with murder! Although Manuel was well received, indeed rapturously in Oporto, on his nineteenth birthday, his return to Constitutionalism resulted in frequent changes of Government, no less than six in his reign of two years and eight months. The alternating political parties were the *Regenerators* who generated nothing and the *Progressives* who made no progress! The Monarchists endeavoured to raise support for the Throne and formed a league[48] but the republicans still thriving, gained control of the City Council of Lisbon. There was growing frustration at the lack of promotion prospects for junior officers in the Army and Navy. Republican agitators attempted to incite the armed services to revolt and they organised civilian gangs of *Carbonários*[49] equipped with weapons. There were endless rumours of conspiracies to overthrow the regime, although it is estimated that the republicans only comprised some seven percent of the actual electorate throughout the nation and there were only fourteen elected republican deputies in the last Monarchist parliament; eleven of these were returned for Lisbon. Manuel's policies favoured strengthening the ancient Alliance with Great Britain and there were rumours about an engagement to Princess Patricia, daughter of the Duke of Connaught, who had visited Portugal in 1905. In 1909, Manuel made a successful and popular State Visit to Great Britain and his name was linked next to Princess Alexandra, daughter of the Duke of Fife but these plans did not materialise.[50]

---

47 - The lengthy police investigation dragged on until the implementation of the Republic on 5 October 1910. Although the dossier was probably destroyed, Dom Pedro d'Avillez has published in *Dossier Regicídio -O processo desparacedio* the conclusions of the autopsies on the cadavers of Buiça and Costa evidence that the bullets which killed the assassins were not of the kind or calibre used by the police nor normally found in Portugal. Hence it is believed that they were shot by other republicans which makes a mockery of their hypocritical sympathy for the assassins

48 - This was the predecessor of *The Monarchist Cause* organisation - *Causa Monárquica* - formed in 1910.

49 - The name came from the early 19th century Italian revolutionary secret society members, who were called *Carbonari* , and whose name and rituals were borrowed from the mutual-aid societies of charcoal burners. Both in Italy and Portugal they were very much under the influence of Freemasons

50 - There was also a suggestion of marriage with Lady Louise Mountbatten(1889-1965), Earl Mountbatten's sister, who married King Gustaf VI Adolf of Sweden in 1923

Dom Manuel II: a King who was enthusiastic in his duties and popular with his people.

Dom Manuel II received with rapture in Oporto on his nineteenth birthday. Anyone witnessing such overt demonstrations of loyalty and popularity would surely have considered the collapse of the Monarchy within two years to be inconceivable. The King stands at the windows of his palace of *Carrancas* that he bequeathed in his will to be converted into a hospital for the sick of Oporto. Today it houses the city's fine art gallery.

The King of Portugal's State Visit to London 17 November 1909
Dom Manuel received an address of welcome from the Mayor of Marylebone at Oxford Circus. Seated next to him in the carriage is the then Prince of Wales, later King George V.

D. Manuel recebendo a mensagem do Mayor de Marylebone em Oxford-Circus

49

Dom Manuel received the Freedom of the City of London and was presented with a gold jewelled casket. The King was invested as a Knight of the Garter, followed by a State Banquet at Windsor. The photographs show his Garter insignia and Dom Manuel delivering his speech at the dinner.

He returned in May 1910 for the funeral of Edward VII when there were nine kings present to pay their respects.

(see Appendix)

Gaby Deslys, Dom Manuel's girl friend

who he met in Paris, on his return journey to Portugal after the State Visit to the United Kingdom in 1909. He accommodated her at Bussaco but she ended up in London kept by Gordon Selfridge, the American millionaire who owned the famous Oxford Street stores. She lived in a house that he provided in Kensington Gore, allegedly smothered in jewels. When she died she left her money to the poor of Marseilles.

On his return from the State Visit, during which he had been honoured with the Most Noble Order of the Garter, Manuel met in Paris an actress, called Gaby Deslys[51] and imported her to Portugal. The liaison was frowned on by many but he kept her at the splendiferous palace at Bussaco. There was medical evidence[52] that six months after they met, he became afflicted with syphilis, which was rampant at the time and incurable.

In March 1910 Manuel's bachelor uncle Afonso, the only other surviving male member of the reigning Royal Family, was declared to be Heir Presumptive. He had served Portugal as Viceroy in India and this was a cautious move to preserve the succession. It may well have been plausible that a couple of well placed pot shots would have exterminated the ruling male line. Yet it was likely that even extremists would have ruled out another assassination attempt because it would have caused their tremendous alienation from the people for their cause. In May 1910, Manuel was the youngest of the nine kings who attended the funeral of King Edward VII and in his letter to his mother, from Buckingham Palace where he stayed, he described this memorable event. (see Appendix)

However, the republicans were determined to undermine the Royal Family. Bribery of highly placed officials was exposed in Parliament, involving the King's adjutant. Then it was disclosed in the Press that Maria Pia, the Dowager Queen Mother, owed a Parisian jeweller a small fortune. Initiations into Masonic Lodges multiplied rapidly and republican Freemasons infiltrated the armed forces, the police, the civil service and even the Royal Household itself, everywhere spreading sedition. The murder of a popular republican member of parliament, director of the Lisbon Lunatic Asylum, killed by one of his own patients who was a Monarchist, provoked the outbreak of the revolution on the night of October 3rd/4th 1910. Two naval cruisers bombarded the Necessidades Palace from the Tagus but Admiral Reis, who ordered the insurrection, believed it had failed and committed suicide. Manuel was in residence and the shells penetrated and damaged some of the state rooms.

----

51 - A biography was published in German in 1920: *Gaby Deslys De Roman einer Tanzerin* by Reinhard Ranf. She ended up being kept in London by Gordon Selfridge, the American stores millionaire and bequeathed her wealth to the poor of Marseilles. *Gaby Deslys - a fatal attraction* by James Gardner was published in 1986 by Sidgwick & Jackson Ltd. ISBN 0-283-99398-7

52 - The diary of his doctor, Thomaz de Mello Breyner for 1908-1910, published in 1992, contains references see entries for 16th and 21st June 1910 re his examination and the treatment of the King.

Drawing of the naval bombardment of the Royal Palace of Necessidades during the night of the 3rd/4th October 1910, whilst Dom Manuel was in residence.

Photographs of the bomb damage to the Palace's rooms.
Dr Miguel Bombarda who treated the mentally deranged and was a popular doctor. He was a Republican and was killed by one of his patients who was a Monarchist; this sparked the outbreak of the Revolution.

Dr. Miguel Bombarda

Vice-Almirante Candido dos Reis

Vice-Admiral Candido dos Reis organised a mutiny in the Portuguese Navy and the attack on the Palace. He believed that the Revolt had failed and committed suicide.

The barricade constructed by revolutionaries on the 4th October 1910 at the top of the Avenida at the Rotunda where Pombal's statue was erected in 1934.

Francisco Correa Herédia, the first and only Viscount of Ribeira Brava, riding down the Avenida with his hat raised in triumph. A former Monarchist turned Republican, he is believed to have provided money for munitions to arm the Revolutionaries. He was assassinated in 1918 by disaffected Republicans.

Sketches of the King travelling from Mafra to Ericeira and sailing to the Royal yacht on 5th October 1910.

Troops faithful to the King, in the *Rossio*, who were cut off from supplies, had to resort to drinking from the fountains in the square. Inset is a photograph of a horse of the loyal Municipal Guard shot down by Republicans.

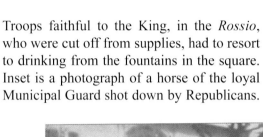

Henrique Armstrong Mitchell de Paiva Couceiro (1861 -1944) cavalry officer, hero of campaigns in Africa, tried to marshal troops loyal to the King when the street fighting broke out in Lisbon 4th October 1910. He commanded the Monarchist incursions of 1911, took a leading role in the incursions of 1912 and proclaimed the restoration of the Monarchy in the North in 1919.

5th October 1910, at about half past three in the afternoon King Manuel II left the shores of Portugal for exile. Dom Manuel is seated in the stern of the first rowing boat whilst his mother and grandmother, the two Queens Amelia and Maria Pia, board the second, to be rowed out to the Royal Yacht anchored off Ericeira, whose population watch from the cliffs above the bay. The people cried out in disbelief *"Your Majesty's not leaving us !"* When the Royal Family reached the yacht, the local rowers raised their oars in a last salutation.

A commemorative plaque, erected there in 1961, reads : *'It was from this beach that on 5th October 1910 the Portuguese Royal Family embarked for exile in the respectful presence of all the population of Ericeira'.*

The King's farewell message (reproduced in part), addressed to António Teixiera de Sousa, the last President of the Council i.e Prime Minister.

Manuel II with King Alfonso XIII of Spain (1886-1941) who was three years older than the King of Portugal. Dom Manuel called him *"Filipe junior"* and he was the grandfather of the present King of Spain Juan Carlos I.

56

Rebel troops surrounded the palace and telegraph wires were cut. Street fighting broke out in Lisbon between the *Carbonários* joined by defectors who had erected barricades across the Rotunda, at the head of the Avenida da Liberdade, and the loyal troops, assembled below on the Rossio. The Monarchist soldiers failed to dislodge the republicans from their barricades, suffered more defections and their officers ordered them to surrender. Manuel left Lisbon on the advice of his Ministers and spent his last night in Portugal at Mafra, where his bedroom is preserved as then. On the 5th October 1910, having been joined by his mother and grandmother who were in Sintra, they travelled to the port of Ericeira to which the Royal Yacht had been brought by his uncle Afonso. Fishermen rowed them out to the anchored yacht and raised their oars in a last salutation. The original plan had been to go north to Oporto which was considered loyal but their way was blocked. So they sailed south to Gibraltar, crossing the estuary of the Tagus with the light-house keepers signalling that their route was clear, as the Republic was implemented through Portugal, ending the Monarchy that had endured throughout eight centuries.

Manuel II sent his noble farewell message which read:

Forced by necessity, I find myself obliged to embark on the Royal Yacht Amélia. I am Portuguese and I shall always be so. I have the conviction of having always done my duty as a King in all circumstances and to have placed my heart and my life at the service of my Country. I hope that convinced of my rights and my dedication, it will be able to recognise this.

Long live Portugal!

After they landed at Gibraltar, the yacht returned to Portugal because, after all, it was State property[53], having been sold back to the Government; furthermore republican repercussions against the crew and their families were avoided. Manuel then decided to come to England with his mother and they sailed from Gibraltar in the British Royal Yacht.

They stayed initially at the home of the Duke of Orleans, Amélia's brother, at Wood Norton, near Evesham. The Republican Government passed a law of banishment against the Royal Family. In January 1911, Manuel and Queen Amélia rented Abercorn House, Richmond[54], Surrey, to be nearer London and the homes of influential Portuguese Monarchists who had followed them into exile.

----

53 - Parts of the yacht have been preserved in the Maritime Museum at Belém; it has been conjectured that the crew had been infiltrated by republicans.

54 - Amélia was born at York House Twickenham in 1865 when her father was in exile from France.

Others left Portugal for Spain where they were made welcome in Galicia, on the northern frontier, where Portuguese is readily understood. The Dowager Queen Mother and Dom Afonso, the Duke of Oporto, went to Italy, where her brother King Umberto I had been assassinated in 1900, as her son and grandson were in 1908. As Maria Pia lay dying on 5th July 1911, her last request was to be turned to face Portugal. Although she remains buried in Italy there are plans for her mortal remains to return to Portugal.

King Alfonso XIII of Spain visited England and came to Richmond to see Manuel II, who used to call him *Filipe Junior* referring to the three Kings of Spain, each called Philip, who had successively ruled Portugal. It has been surmised that there were plans for Spain to intervene in Portugal whose Republican regime was seen as a threat. Spain had already been a republic from 1873 to 1875 and had suffered three years of anarchy. It is believed that, rather than see his native land under Spanish turmoil, Manuel encouraged the British Government to recognise officially the Republic of Portugal nearly one year after he had left. Those who had come to power in Portugal were in the main old men who had struggled against the establishment for decades. The church's properties were appropriated, religious orders expelled and the Cardinal-Patriarch of Lisbon had left the country. Financial crises, shortage of food and unemployment led to the country's first serious strikes and persecutions swept across the land. To the Government's embarrassment, the Royalists still were a powerful threat to the Republic, especially in the North. Numerous Monarchists were arrested, particularly in Braga. Manuel sent £10,000 for the Portuguese emigrants in Galicia.

The Monarchists strike back:

On the first anniversary of the outbreak of the republican revolution, on the 4th October 1911, Monarchist troops invaded Portugal across the northern Spanish frontier. This first incursion was led by Henrique Armstrong Mitchell de Paiva Couceiro (1861-1944), whose mother was English. Formerly a captain in the regular Portuguese Army and a hero of campaigns in Africa, he had tried to marshal the troops loyal to the King when the street fighting broke out in Lisbon. He then demanded that, at least, the new republican regime should hold a plebiscite but when this was refused, he resigned from the Army and left Portugal.

Heartily welcomed in each village, the Monarchists marched with a blue and white flag, but curiously without the Royal Crown, to denote neutrality. This flag had been blessed in Paris with the Duke of Oporto at the ceremony and the standard bearer kept the flag furled so that the omission was not obvious. Although awaited in Braganza itself, where local Monarchists had damaged the armaments of the Republican garrison, tactics were changed. On the actual first anniversary day, the 5th October 1911, of the proclamation of the Republic the Monarchists took the small town of Vinhais, where the regicide Buiça had been born, a parish priest's illegitimate son. The blue and white Royalist flag, provided by a local law clerk, once again fluttered above the town hall and the people shouted *Vivas* for the Monarchy whilst the rest of the population of Portugal was required to celebrate the Republic's first birthday. The Assembly of the Republic went into emergency session, inciting the populace against the revolt and denying constitutional rights to any collaborator, the very same action that had provoked the Regicide in 1908. Couceiro wisely ordered his troops to retreat back into Spain. An anxious Manuel, concerned about the alleged neutrality of the incursion, sent a negative message of prevarication to the despair of his loyal supporters.

The first assembly of the Republic was comprised of several separate republican factions who could not agree on what sanctions to apply to the overt and covert Monarchist population of Portugal. The Prime Minister rebuked them during debate, pointing out that at least in the former times of the Monarchy when national security was threatened, opposed political parties used to unite and agree on a national defence strategy. The build-up of Monarchist troops in Galicia had been well publicised in the Portuguese Press and large numbers of regular forces and reserves, both soldiers and sailors had been sent to the Northern frontier during the summer of 1911, together with *Carbonários* and other republican civilian volunteers. Spanish republicans had been instrumental in detecting the transportation of the armaments sent to the Portuguese in Spain which were seized by the Spanish Guards. The Portuguese Republic's first Minister of War believed that no invasion would take place and withdrew troops from the frontier. However, Couceiro was determined to invade, if necessary unarmed. He believed the local Monarchists would rise to support him and deliberately chose the 4th/5th October 1911, the first anniversary of the implementation of the Republic, as an appropriate day.

The First Monarchist Incursion, 4th/5th October 1911:

Postage stamps printed by the Legitimists in 1911, depicting patriotic scenes and the busts of Dom Miguel I and Dom Miguel (II), ready for use in the event of victory but this was not forthcoming.

Armaments which were destined for Portuguese Monarchists in Galicia, impounded by the Spanish authorities.

Women from the mountain villages flung into prison for greeting the invading Monarchists with *"Vivas"*. The original caption of the photograph depicts them shouting from inside the cell that *"the bread's not too hard in here"*. Retaliatory arrests at Vinhais and a band of Republicans with the parish priest, the Reverend Buiça, who had fathered the illegitimate Regicide, and his orphaned grand-daughter Elvira, grasping the Republic's new flag.

The first incursion was a cleverly calculated gesture, albeit dismissed as a failure by the Republic: nevertheless both sides were losers. The *Carbonários* had a field day, rounding up as prisoners anyone they chose to suspect of being Monarchist; their activities disgusted people of moderate opinion whatever party. The Prime Minister announced that it was believed that about a third of those arrested were innocent and would be released without trial.

The Republic's Government were so concerned that Spain would seize on any pretext to invade Portugal that their troops were ordered to stay inside Portugal, well away from the Spanish frontier. The Republic's troops mobilised against the Monarchists were furious, as they considered themselves to have been prevented from doing a proper job. Couceiro's men had been able to manoeuvre along the frontier with very few casualties although the anticipated uprising of support did not happen and some two thousand Monarchist prisoners were sent to Lisbon.

The entire cabinet threatened to resign unless the Minister of War, who had misled them, went out of office; he was replaced by the Chief of Police. The Prime Minister then announced that the *Carbonários* would be disbanded and renamed *Defensores da República* i.e *Defenders of the Republic* who were paid the equivalent of six shillings a day, then far more than a workman could earn, for surveillance, rooting out and denouncing suspected Monarchists.

Meanwhile the Monarchist troops rested, re-organised and re-armed in Galicia. In the first year of the birth pangs of the Republic, the floating national debt increased by eleven percent, from £18 million at the the end of the Monarchy to £20 million; it then spiralled to over £100 million!

On the 30th January 1912, a momentous historic meeting which lasted two hours took place at the Lord Warden Hotel, Dover, between the Ex-King Dom Manuel II and Dom Miguel (II), only son of the deposed King Dom Miguel I (1802-66), accompanied by his eldest son Prince Miguel, together with their closest advisers, including Couceiro, who was in written communication with Dom Manuel. This meeting was of the utmost dynastic importance to the Braganza family and represented a formal rapprochement between the two branches, seventy-eight years after the Convention of Évora Monte in 1834 had resulted in Dom Miguel I going into exile.

The Second Monarchist Incursion, 8ᵗʰ July 1912: the chapel of Our Lady of the Miracles where the bells were rung, after the invading Monarchists hoisted the Royal Flag, at Vila Verde de Raia; the fort of *São Neutel* at Chaves which was attacked by Couceiro's forces, from the bluff called Mount *Espaldão* (lit. large back of a chair) at the rear, across the firing carriage-way outside the fort; the distant mountains mark the Spanish frontier crossed by the invaders on the night before. The photographs were taken in 1912 and 1999.

Bugler António d'Azevedo and his son, who raised the alarm, when he saw the invaders, during his early morning milk round.
Unidentified bodies of Monarchists who gave their lives for the Royalist Cause.

No formal protocol was issued, although there were subsequent attempts to formulate what had been agreed. However, Dom Miguel (II) wrote down the following in his own hand, in Portuguese, French and German, for a Press release: *Last Tuesday, Dom Manuel was in Dover to meet his cousin Dom Miguel. On this occasion the two Senhors promised to employ their forces in common to free the beloved homeland from the very sad situation in which it found itself.*

At the beginning of July 1912, the second incursion was launched from Galicia and was a much more serious and devastating blow to both sides than the first had been in 1911. There were several attacking columns; the largest with Couceiro, in a master stroke of strategy, appeared before Montalegre, which caused the Republic's troops to leave Chaves, an important garrison town some twenty miles away. Meanwhile, another column took Vila Verde da Raia, a small township, just over the frontier, north of Chaves and the Monarchist flag again fluttered once more over a Portuguese community. The Republic's cavalry had left Chaves in an attempt to oust the Royalists from Vila Verde. Couceiro's troops marched overnight to Chaves from where nearly every soldier, except those in the regimental band, had hurried to Montalegre or Vila Verde. A boy, son of a bugler, was delivering milk on his early morning round, when he discovered the arrival of the Royalist forces and he gave the alarm. Every civilian republican in Chaves rushed to man the guns in the fortress and succeeded in driving back the invaders, firing some 49,000 cartridges with an average of 1,300 shots falling around each attacker! These two columns of invaders were badly co-ordinated and failed to join up.

In the Minho, several towns declared the restoration of the Monarchy but only briefly, as the Republic mobilised over 5,500 men and sent troops north. Revolts also broke out in other parts but all the insurrections and invasions were quelled with considerable loss of life. Others were wounded and many were taken prisoner, yet Couceiro and most of his forces managed to escape back into Spain.

It had cost the Portuguese Government about £440,000 and, at the end of July, they welcomed Spanish republican leaders in Lisbon. This time, Ex-King Manuel II sent a suitable message to his valiant surviving adherents, acknowledging their courage and proclaiming that the Monarchist Cause had not died with their defeat.

The marriage of Dom Manuel and his second cousin, Auguste Viktoria, daughter of Wilhelm Prince of Hohenzollern on the 4th September 1913. The wedding guests included Edward, the then young Prince of Wales, seen at the far left hand side of this photograph taken in the gardens of the Castle at Sigmaringen. Next to him is the Dowager Grand Duchess of Baden; by Dom Manuel stands Queen Amèlia and on the right of the group is the exiled Cardinal Patriarch of Lisbon.

The Infanta Maria Antónia(1845 - 1913), Dom Manuel's great-aunt and Princess Auguste Viktoria's grandmother. The photograph was taken in 1861 which was the year that she married Prince Leopold of Hohenzollern. Her grand-daughter wore the wedding veil of her Portuguese grandmother who was too frail to attend the celebrations.

Queen Augusta Vitória wearing the insignia of the Order of Saint Isabel.

This second incursion was supported by the Governments of Spain, Austria and Germany but it is believed that the young Republic of Portugal had the veiled support of Great Britain and the British Intelligence Service! Monarchist prisoners awaiting trial were held for months, some over a year, in dark, damp, cramped, filthy, verminous subterranean cells. Those sentenced to the further horrors of solitary confinement were treated like the worst convicts and compelled to wear the *cagoule*, a resurrected punishment which had been abolished in Portugal in the previous century. It comprised a heavy hooded shroud with two slits for eye holes and debarment from all speech. However the plight of the political prisoners was highlighted in 1913 by a published 'British national protest' led by the Earl of Lytton, the Duchess of Bedford and the Hon. Aubrey Herbert, M.P. In March 1914, the President of the Republic granted an amnesty to all those Monarchists who were still serving sentences of imprisonment and they were released. In other words, the Republic behaved exactly like the Monarchy had done, when republicans used to be imprisoned and then subsequently freed. In later times the State recognised the ideals of each side in naming in Lisbon, both a street in memory of 'The Defenders of Chaves' and a large square to immortalise the bravery of Paiva de Couceiro.

The marriage of the Ex-King:

In April 1913, Manuel II was engaged to Auguste Viktoria, Princess of Hohenzollern ; they were second cousins through her grandmother and his great-aunt, the Infanta Dona Antónia, who had married in 1861 Leopold, Prince of Hohenzollern. Manuel proposed marriage within half an hour of first meeting her but the match had been previously arranged by Queen Amélia and Augusta's father Wilhelm, Prince of Hohenzollern. They were both twenty-three years old and the wedding took place in great splendour at Sigmaringen on the 4th September 1913. Although her grandmother was too frail to attend the wedding which was celebrated by the exiled Cardinal Patriarch of Lisbon, the bride wore Princess Antónia's veil, conserved from her wedding fifty-two years past.

The Portuguese emigrants in Galicia gave a rich edition of the classic epic *Os Lusíadas* by Camões, wrapped in the Royalist flag that flew over Vila Verde in 1912. Over five thousand telegrams of congratulations arrived at Sigmaringen from Portugal, together with many lavish presents, including a magnificent gold model of a *caravela,* the famed Portuguese sailing vessel.

Fulwell Park, Twickenham

King Manuel's study with his furniture from Portugal ; fresh flowers from the garden were arranged on his desk each day by Queen Augusta ; the bibliophile King worked here with Miss Marjorie Withers, cataloguing 16th century Portuguese books.

Manuel wore the insignia of the Order of the Garter and Edward, then the young Prince of Wales, later briefly King Edward VIII and subsequently Duke of Windsor, represented Great Britain. Their honeymoon was planned for the Black Forest but Augusta became seriously ill and she had to be hospitalised in Munich, with an alleged kidney infection.

The Royal couple resided at Fulwell Park, Twickenham and the Queen Mother, Amélia decided to return to reside in her native France. The house was furnished with the exiled King's private property from the Royal palaces in Portugal. This was acceptable to the Portuguese Government which also granted Dom Manuel a monthly allowance of some £1,100. In August 1914 the First World War erupted and Portugal did not mobilise until 1916 but then naturally on the side of the Allies. The ex-King instructed his representative in Portugal to write to the President formally to express his willingness to serve his Country in the Portuguese Army. Manuel offered his services to the British Red Cross and his wife, although German born, wanted to work as a nurse in a London hospital.

The King and Queen were well thought of in the Richmond area and Manuel, who took a lively interest in local affairs, was much in demand. They worshipped regularly at St James' Roman Catholic church, Pope's Grove, Strawberry Hill and were popular godparents. The church treasures their donations of silver communion cruets and a ciborium marked with the King's monogram and a baptismal shell. In 1932 King Manuel resolved to mark the 700th anniversary of the death of St. Anthony of Lisbon and Padua by dedicating two windows in memory of Canon English, the parish priest who died in 1924. The stained glass, designed by Anthony Orr, displays the Royal arms of Portugal with the inscription *Santo António de Lisboa, rogas por nós = St Anthony of Lisbon pray for us*. A contemporary worshipper had recollections of Augusta often in tears. She was a keen gardener and daily arranged the flowers for his study.

The ex-King attended the annual services at Windsor for the Knights of the Order of the Garter and was a tennis enthusiast, frequently as a player and also as a spectator during the Wimbledon matches. His widow donated King Manuel's organ to the church as she left Fulwell Park which was sold in 1934 and demolished. A housing estate was built on the site and the roads commemorate their sojourn ie. Manoel Road, Augusta Road, Lisbon Avenue, Portugal Gardens and Fulwell Park Avenue.

The church of St. James, Pope's Grove, Twickenham where the King in exile worshipped for seventeen years

Two fine stained glass windows at the front of the church were donated by the King in memory of Canon Michael English, the parish priest who had died in 1924. Dom Manuel resolved to mark the 700th anniversary(1932) of the death of St. Anthony of Lisbon and Padua. The stained glass, designed by Anthony Orr, displays the Royal arms of Portugal with the inscription *Santo António de Lisboa, rogas por nós = St Anthony of Lisbon pray for us.*

The church treasures their donations of silver communion cruets, a ciborium marked with the King's monogram and a baptismal shell. Queen Augusta also gave the church Dom Manuel's organ when she left Fulwell Park.
She remarried in 1939 and went to live in Germany.

The *prie-dieux* believed to have been used by the King and Queen when they prayed in the side chapel

The names of the roads of the
housing estate built on the site
of the demolished Fulwell Park
record the King's sojourn

The Infante Dom Afonso, Duke of Oporto (1865 - 1920) with his mother, Queen Maria Pia, and his wife, Nevada Stoody Hayes.
The silver casket that contained his coffin in the Royal Pantheon, prior to 1932 and the Duchess of Oporto in mourning. Vada was then fifty but only admitted to thirty-five years of age.

The marriage of the Duke of Oporto:

In 1917 the Portuguese Monarchists suffered another dynastic shock when Dom Afonso, Duke of Oporto married in Rome, at the Methodist church, the previously thrice married American Nevada Stoody Hayes. He was still the heir to Dom Manuel II, whose marriage of four years was childless and the ex-King then cut his uncle out of his will. This American opportunist, who was twice divorced, had inherited a substantial sum from her second husband who was reputed to have been worth some twenty million U.S.dollars. She had married him, forty years her senior, on the day of her divorce from her first husband but her second died sixteen months later. Nevada then married a wealthy lawyer and although their marriage was stormy and short lived, she received a prodigious divorce settlement. Although she was only five years younger than the Duke of Oporto, she lyingly subtracted fifteen years from her age and pretended she was considerably younger than she actually was. Her maiden name was really Sarah (known as Sadie) Nevada Stoody. She was born in 1870, not 1885 as she stated; she had dropped the Sarah/Sadie, was known as Vada and seems to have added Hayes, from her second husband's names. After Afonso's death, in 1920 in Italy, where they lived, his body was taken to Portugal by an Italian warship and buried in a silver casket in the Pantheon. The Duchess also came to Portugal and gave interviews to the Portuguese press. In 1921 she ghosted his biography with no mention of her three previous marriages, implying that Afonso and she had been long time sweethearts! Nevada recorded that he treasured the handful of earth which he had taken from Portugal in 1910, when the Royal Family went into exile on the Royal Yacht.

She quoted the words of his favourite Portuguese refrain:
Two kisses I hold in my soul, that will never leave me: my mother's last and the first that you gave me When the Duchess died in Florida in 1941, she left money to cover the cost of her internment in the Pantheon but the Portuguese Government would not allow it.

The restoration of the Monarchy in the North:

In 1918 Sidónio Pais became President after a coup and in a General Election, the Monarchists secured 39 seats in Parliament whilst the Republicans held 106. Invariably, elections were rigged in favour of the Republic. A disastrous year in the annals of Portugal followed; there was an extreme left wing revolt against the Government and then the assassination of the President.

The Restoration of the Monarchy in the North in January 1919 :

The Orders issued by Dom Manuel's surrogate-lieutenant in Portugal headed, in English, *"Go on !"*

The proclamation of the restoration from the balconies of the Council Hall of Viana do Castelo on 23rd January 1919.

Postage stamps and fiscal stamps for stamp duty issued and used during the Restoration.

The Eden Theatre in Oporto depicted after the building had been attacked by Republicans, showing (1) where the 'infernal' piano was played by Esmeralda Vilar (photograph) whilst Republicans were tortured on stage; (2) the trapdoors beneath which prisoners here held; (3) the boxes where masked Monarchists encouraged the torments. Instruments of torture, including a blood stained handkerchief of a former priest, Camilo de Oliviera, who became a Republican, displayed afterwards in an Oporto shop window. Paiva Couceiro's hat left behind in the Monarchist Government's headquarters at Oporto.

Taking advantage of the weakness of the State, the staunch inde-fatigable Couceiro proclaimed in Oporto, on the 19th January 1919, the restoration of the Monarchy. The Monarchist flag was raised above the main barracks and the Royalist National Anthem was played in public again. Simultaneously, the restoration of Dom Manuel II to the throne of Portugal was proclaimed from the balconies of the town halls of important cities in the North. The Minister of War travelled swiftly from Lisbon to Oporto to try to persuade the troops to switch back their allegiance but was promptly arrested in the barracks of the 'Republican' Guard! A provi-sional government was set up in the name of King Manuel II, and the Monarchy was restored throughout the whole of the North, as far south as Viseu.

Meanwhile Monarchist troops attacked the fort on the heights of Monsanto, outside Lisbon on Saint Vincent's day , hoisting their flag there on the 23rd January. The Government troops, with ten thousand enlisted volunteers, surrounded the fort, whilst the Monarchists fired shells on them towards Lisbon. Fortunately the civilian population was spared but one shot landed in the zoo and a poor chimpanzee was wounded in the hand. The fort was quickly regained by the republicans and ten Monarchists were killed in the fighting, with twenty-three more wounded.

The Cabinet resigned, and a new Government was formed from all the republican factions with the intention of wiping out the 'Monarchy of the North'. Heavy fines were imposed on all the communities which had proclaimed the Restoration and fifteen thousand troops were dispatched to the North, where the Republic was re-established on 13th February. Prison sentences of fifteen years were imposed on those captured who had held office in the Monarchist Provisional Government but the 'Portuguese Pimpernel', Couceiro, had managed to escape over the Spanish frontier.
The restored 'Monarchy of the North' had been doomed by two insur-mountable set-backs i.e. the Spanish Government's prevention of gun-run-ning over the border, in spite of the large stocks of armaments that the Portuguese Monarchists held in Spain and an apparent lack of enthusias-tic support from King Manuel himself. It was believed that he had given tacit approval but there was a dearth of direct communication between the King and his adherents who were bitter that he had not wholeheartedly welcomed their brave endeavours nor indeed returned to his native land.

The republicans lost no opportunity in issuing much anti-monarchist propaganda. Particularly nasty were the allegations of torture inflicted on republican prisoners held under the trapdoor of the stage of the Eden Theatre in Oporto, where previously Monarchists had been imprisoned. It was claimed that Monarchists had sat masked in their boxes, watching the tortures on stage, to the accompaniment of music played on an 'infernal' piano, although Couceiro had issued orders that all prisoners were to be treated leniently. However the Monarchists contradicted by stating that Esmeralda Vilar could not even play the piano and that the blood displayed had come from an abattoir.

In 1921, following an all-night sitting in Parliament when the votes were 50 in favour and 22 against, the Republican Government granted an amnesty to, and freed from prison, those who had been sentenced for taking part in the 1919 uprisings.

The formation of *the New State*:

In 1911, 1 Escudo = 1,625.85 milligrams of fine gold and £1 Sterling = 4.5 Escudos. By 1924, the Escudo had depreciated during thirteen years by a staggering 97%! In other words if you had saved your money in the national Portuguese currency during the lifetime of the First Republic, it would have been worth only 3% of the original value. Between 1910 and 1926 there were some forty-five changes of government, with numerous attempted *coupes d'état,* plots and insurrections. In October 1921, the ex- prime minister and two cabinet ministers of the fallen Government were killed. Admiral Machado dos Santos, revolutionary hero of the fighting in 1910 at the Rotunda and founding father of the Republic, was arrested and murdered in cold blood by his guard. Of ten presidents, only two had terms of office as long as four years. The average term of an administration endured six months; one only lasted ten days. It was obvious that Portugal was suffering from the most serious political and grave economic instability; national bankruptcy was again imminent.

With the support of distinguished national figures of standing, including avowed Monarchists, on 28th May 1926 the Military instituted the *Estado Novo i.e. the New State* with the eventual effect of the abolition of any political freedom left in Portugal, but aiming to save the Nation from political anarchy and economic collapse.

This overthrow of the previous regime did provide the possibility of the restoration of the Monarchy and, moreover, Dom Manuel's former Surrogate Lieutenant in Portugal, Coutinho, had been elected to the Senate, the upper chamber of Parliament. It was his son who had carried the flag in the 1911 incursion. However it was resolved that the time was not yet ripe for a restoration and although the republican regime continued, there was no prohibition on a Monarchist holding political office.

The Military, of course, had not the faintest practical idea of how to rectify the appalling financial mess, and in 1928, Dr.Salazar, an academic accountant and economist at Coimbra University, joined the government as Finance Minister. The currency was eventually stabilised on the basis of :1 Escudo = 66.57 milligrams of fine gold and £1 Sterling = 110 Escudos i.e the Pound was worth over twenty-four times more than its value when compared with the Escudo in 1911. After balancing the books, Salazar became prime minister in 1932 and the lynch pin of the regime. Although he never took the office of President, he was the *de facto* dictator of Portugal until incapacitated in 1968; Salazar died in 1970.

The last of the Constitutional Monarchs:

For the last eight years, Manuel, who was a keen bibliophile and recognised to be a distinguished scholar, had devoted himself to the meticulous production of an elaborate catalogue, in both Portuguese and English, of the early printed Portuguese books in his library, those from 1489 to 1600. The King was helped considerably in his painstaking efforts by his dedicated librarian Miss Margery Withers. The reason for this considerable undertaking was movingly set out in His Majesty's introduction to the first volume of the catalogue :

In trying to give life to these early Portuguese books... we seek to bring into relief the achievements of the Portuguese, especially in the fifteenth and sixteenth centuries...The purpose of our work is to show the greatness of the Portuguese exploits, and to serve our nation by raising 'the banner of her triumphs. It is unpretentious, says nothing new and does not presume to teach anyone, but we hope that it will prove our love for our country; if we achieve that ambition, we shall have the supreme consolation of a duty done

Frontispiece of a rare Portuguese book, from Dom Manuel II's library, printed in the reign of Dom Manuel I *The Fortunate,* depicting his badge of an armillary sphere. The book plate of Dom Manuel II *The Unfortunate,* based on the heraldic devices of his predecessor, together with his motto *"Depois de Vós Nós = After You Us".*

The statue in the Pantheon of *O Dor = Grief,* by Francisco Franco, representing Portugal weeping over the bodies of her martyred King and Crown Prince.

The bust of Dom Manuel II made by Barrata Feyo in gilt bronze in 1982, fifty years after the King's death. It now graces the National Library in Lisbon to honour the great bibliophile King.

Manuel, in his adolescence, had learned to play the organ with skill and he was well educated. The rigorous timetable of studies starting at 7 a.m., drawn up to prepare him for entry into the Navy on merit, must have stood him in good stead for kingship. English history books tend to be dismissive of his short reign and treat him as an inept boy ruler. A careful political study of his time in Portugal shows that he did well to last as long as he did, surrounded as he was by the treacherous and the incompetent. There can be no doubt that he placed his country's interests beyond his own. He is deemed to be a true patriot and an intelligent and noble King by most Portuguese historians. Certainly his unselfish policies in exile prevented civil war and consequential bloodshed. Salazar went on record as saying that the political policies of Dom Manuel centred on three fundamental axioms, to which he himself fully subscribed : first, the liberty and absolute independence of Portugal; second, the Anglo-Portuguese Alliance as a basis of Portuguese external political policy and third, the unity of the Portuguese nation to be placed above all divisions and all political interests should be in the cause of the Nation. In 1988, President Mário Soares, formerly Socialist Prime Minister of Portugal was the first Head of the Portuguese State to dine at the exclusive Oporto Factory House of the Port Wine shippers, since King Manuel II dined there in 1908. In his speech, President Soares said that Dom Manuel was a King for whom he had the highest respect and indeed admiration for his enlightened political views.

Manuel died through lack of medical attention; needlessly, and in horrendous agony. He was prone to throat infections; his doctor's diary records that on 17th December 1908 he went to hospital to lance an abscess in the King's throat to release a large quantity of pus. On the 1st July 1932 Manuel was worried about a fierce pain in his larynx and telephoned the personal physician of King George V, Lord Dawson who advised complete rest. Dawson became so notorious for his poor diagnoses and treatments that he is commemorated in the following couplet *Lord Dawson of Penn killed so many men!* As Manuel was no better the next day, he was driven to London to see the famous laryngologist, Sir Malcolm Reed, who did not suspect the imminent tragedy and Manuel returned to Fulwell Park, at about 1 30 pm in a worsening condition. In desperate ignorance, the Queen applied compresses to his throat that proved fatal.

The late King's widow and mother leave Westminster Cathedral after Solemn Requiem Mass. The mortal remains of ex-King Dom Manuel II were taken back to Portugal on HMS Concord, commanded by Captain Ardill R.N. As the battleship entered the Tagus the Portuguese Royal standard was hoisted and flew again for the first time since twenty-two years previous when the flag was bombarded, flying outside the Royal Palace, at the outbreak of the Republican Revolution. As the ship berthed by *Black Horse Square*, the Portuguese Royal Standard was lowered and then placed over the coffin, then carried ashore by British Sailors, as the Last Post was played by a trumpeter of the Royal Marines. Below the flag, and directly behind the coffin, was the Viscount d' Asseca, former chamberlain to the King, who had accompanied Dom Manuel when he left in the Royal Yacht in 1910 and had stayed in England with his Sovereign. Inset is a photograph taken before 1908, showing the two princes taking exercise, riding out of the Royal Palace with the Viscount d' Asseca, after their daily routine of lessons.

Gasping for breath he asked for a crucifix which he kissed in agony. He choked to death, age forty-two, at 2 30 p.m., on Saturday, 2nd July, in the presence of his wife and his Portuguese private secretary. Manuel's last words, spoken with his final breath were that he was the last Portuguese Monarch. The death certificate records under Cause of death as registered on the 5th July: Acute Inflammation and Oedema (i.e. swelling) of the Glottis (i.e. opening of wind pipe), Acute Inflammation of the left Tonsil and left side of Pharynx; Asphyxia (i..e. suffocation) ; no P.(ost) M.(ortem); certified by Milsom Rees F.(Fellow of) R.(the Royal) C.(College)S.(of Surgeons). Reed arrived at Fulwell Park to find a dead patient and was criticised for not having foreseen the crisis, when a tracheotomy (incision into the wind pipe) could have saved the King. All sorts of rumours began to circulate such as Manuel was only prepared to allow a Portuguese doctor to make the incision that could have been equally fatal and that his throat had been swollen by quinsy, that could have been freed by penknife to relieve the breathing but his entourage were too frightened to try. It is inconceivable that either his wife or secretary would have known how to take this extreme measure, particularly following the so called expert advice received earlier that day. The King was very run down before his death, constantly complaining of fatigue when compiling the catalogue and extremely worried about his precarious financial position, although some agreements had been reached with the Portuguese Government regarding the ex-King's private property in Portugal. Manuel would not have had the natural resistance to fight the infection. In those days antibiotics, that could have reduced the swelling and infection, were unknown. Furthermore, investigative probing during the medical examination could have worsened the condition. It was amazing that Reed did not admit Manuel into hospital to have the position monitored and where his life could have been easily saved.

Queen Amélia, on arriving at Twickenham, cried *he was the last thing I had* and after a private Mass at Fulwell Park, the King's body was moved to St. Charles Borromeo, Weybridge, which was originally a private Roman Catholic Chapel. The casket was then taken to Westminster Cathedral for a Solemn Requiem Mass, in the presence of the late Duke of Gloucester, representing his father King George V, Manuel's widow and his mother, the Portuguese Ambassador and the exiled King Alfonso XIII of Spain. The cortège went through Twickenham, past St. James' Church, where the King had worshipped.

As the Royal Marines' contingent present arms, the mortal remains of Dom Manuel, covered by the Portuguese Royal Standard, were carried onto Portuguese soil. Behind the coffin, next to the Viscount d' Asseca was the ex-King's valet, António Pereira, who held Queen Dona Augusta Vitória's floral tribute from the garden at Fulwell Park.

The British sailors hand over the King's coffin to the Portuguese, headed by the greatly honoured João d'Azevedo Coutinho, Dom Manuel's last Surrogate-Lieutenant in Portugal.

Eight Portuguese Monarchists then carried the body of their King. They were former officers who led the Monarchist Incursions in 1911 and 1912: Silveira Ramos, Sáturio Pires, Delfim Maia, António Lobo de Vasconcelos, Lopo Vaz de Sampaio e Melo, Seabra de Lacerda, Júlio da Costa Pinto and Ribeiro de Menezes.

His body then was laid in St. Charles Borromeo's Church where so many relatives of Queen Amélia had been buried, including King Louis Philippe and most of his descendants who died in exile, until such time as their bodies could be transferred for re-burial in France.

The Royal Navy returned the body of King Manuel II to Portugal on 'HMS Concord' flying the Portuguese Royal Standard, passing the King's palace overlooking the Tagus, where the Standard had last flown in 1910. The vessel was escorted by two Portuguese battleships and berthed by *Black Horse Square*. The flag was lowered and placed over the coffin by the Viscount d'Asseca, who had borne the train of the Royal mantle at the King's acclamation ceremony in 1908. The King's valet, António Pereira held flowers, chosen by his widow from the garden of Fulwell Park, and there were also floral tributes from his mother and King George V and Queen Mary which were put on top of the coffin. As buglers of the Royal Marines sounded the 'Last Post', British sailors carried the King's body on to Portuguese soil. The King's mortal remains were placed on a catafalque and received by João d'Azevedo Coutinho, the King's Surrogate-Lieutenant in Portugal, escorted by eight former officers who had fought in the incursions of 1911 and 1912. It is a Portuguese tradition that when the Head of a Noble House dies, the coat of arms, carved in stone, above the doorway, is covered in black crêpe. Throughout Lisbon all public buildings with the Portuguese escutcheon, still surmounted by the Royal Crown, displayed the armorial bearings draped in this manner. The funeral procession was led by the Vicar-General of the Patriarchy and Queen Amélia's former confessor. Eight Portuguese sailors carried the body to *Black Horse Square* and placed the coffin on a gun carriage which passed through the streets of Lisbon with full military honours. The King's mortal remains were laid to rest with those of his forebears in the Pantheon at St Vincent's in the presence of the Portuguese Government, including Salazar and the President of the Republic, the British Ambassador and the forever faithful Paiva Couceiro.

The epitaph on his tomb reads appropriately:

Here rests with God
The King Dom Manuel II
who died in exile having served his country well

Eight Portuguese sailors bore the coffin to *Black Horse Square,* led by three priests who were the Vicar General of the Patriarchy, Canon Anaquim, his colleague, Damasceno Fiadeiro, who had been Queen Amélia's confessor, and the master of ceremonies Father Honorato Monteiro. The sailors were Virgílio Costa Pereira, Manuel Mota Freire, Leopoldo Narciso Gomes, António Santos Lima, João Almeida, José Moreira, José Silva & José Francisco. Their colleagues formed a guard of honour with rifles point downwards in a funeral salute.

Black Horse Square, 2nd August 1932 ; the coffin that contained the mortal remains of Dom Manuel II was borne on a gun carriage, escorted around the square and then to St. Vincent's, given full honours by the Republic's Cavalry, Infantry and Navy, whilst the streets of Lisbon were crowded with Portuguese who had come to pay their respects to their unfortunate last King.

The coffin of Ex-King Dom Manuel II, passed the place of the Regicide, covered by the Portuguese Royal Standard and floral tributes from his widow, his mother and King George V and Queen Mary.

Outside St. Vincent's, the Portuguese Government of the 'New State' awaited the arrival of the Royal cortège. In the centre was the new President of the Council (Prime Minister) Dr. Salazar. Inside the church, amongst the distinguished mourners was he who had fought so valiantly for the King's rights and the return in his life time, that was not to be, the seventy-two years old Henrique Paiva Couceiro.

Dom Manuel's tomb bearing the inscription
"Here rests with God The King Dom Manuel II who died in exile having served his country well."
In 1995 the Association in the United Kingdom of the Order of Saint Michael of the Wing restored the marble crown on the tomb in memory of the King's exile in England

Portuguese women knelt in the streets of Lisbon in 1951, as the coffin of Queen Amélia passed the place of the Regicide, forty-three years before.

Her funeral at St Vincent's was attended by the President, Dr Salazar, and the Patriarch of Lisbon. Shop windows displayed tributes in her memory and the crowds, waiting to pay their respects, queued outside the church all the way up to Graça.

Six months after Dom Manuel died, probate was granted to his executors, Messrs Coutts, bankers and the value of his effects in England was £26,447 11s 6d. His will had been made in 1915 two years after his marriage and had only been altered by the codicil of 1919 depriving his uncle of his legacy, by reason of Manuel's disapproval of his marriage. Certain of the provisions having been made some twenty years earlier could not be exactly complied with and, as Manuel was at that time negotiating for agreement with the Portuguese Government as to what was his private property, as opposed to that belonging to the State, there were surprising omissions. Only three specific properties are named and these had been purchased privately by his immediate predecessors. He wanted a museum of the House of Braganza, to be formed from the Royal collections. His palace in Oporto is now the City's main Art Gallery, with the main road in front named after him. The Portuguese Government formed a trust, called the Foundation of the House of Braganza to administer the Ducal Palace at Vila Viçosa and other possessions, from which initially there were revenues. An agricultural study centre has been established in the Alentejo region, named after his father.

His much loved mother Queen Amélia made an official visit to Portugal in 1945 and died, aged eighty-six in France in 1951. Her body came back to Portugal for burial in the Pantheon. As her coffin passed the place of the regicide, forty-three years before, women knelt in the street in prayer and the crowds wept in memory of so brave a Queen, who had there lost her husband and eldest son, hurling her bouquet at the assassin to save her younger boy. The inscription on her tomb reads:

Here rests with God Queen Dona Amélia of Orleans and Braganza who reigned with kindness and in sorrow.

In 1982 a special Mass was said in St. Vincent's on the fiftieth anniversary of his death and commemorations were held in Portugal in 1989 to mark the centenary of his birth. A fine bust of Dom Manuel II adorns the National Library in Lisbon to acknowledge the great bibliographer King. The last King of Portugal was above party ideologies; a kind monarch who could bear no ill will to his own people. His illustrious predecessor, Manuel I, was described as *The Fortunate*, so it was appropriate that Manuel II became styled ***The Unfortunate***.

Appendix: The text of a letter written by King Manuel II from Buckingham Palace to Queen Amelia, his mother, on the occasion of the funeral of King Edward VII

Translation by Margery Withers, M.B.E. -formerly the King's librarian

"Darling Mother,

You must have already received my two postcards. We had an excellent journey, first from Lisbon to Paris. At the Spanish frontier, Guarda, Villar Formoso and Fuentes de Ouro it was so cold that it was necessary to light the heaters in the carriages. Afterwards in France, successively sunshine, lots of rain and thunder and lightening. We arrived late because of the derailment of a train ahead of us. At the station in Paris were the whole Legation and lots of people and the Infanta Eulalia[1], who had much to ask about you, mother. We left Paris yesterday morning for Calais at a vertiginous speed and embarked for Dover, where we also arrived very late because of a terrible "fogg" in the Channel. It was extremely unpleasant; we nearly ran into another ship, but fortunately it did not happen.

I found Soveral[2] very frail and low; he asked a lot about you, mother. In London I was met at the station by the King[3] and the whole royal family; and there were masses of people on the streets from Victoria Station to the Palace. When we arrived here the King introduced me to the whole household and took me straight up to Queen Alexandra[4]. When she saw me she embraced me in tears. Poor darling: I feel so sorry for her. She asked after my dear mother with the greatest tenderness and concern. We talked for a while and in the end the King put his arms around me at one side and Queen Alexandra on the other, and the King said to the Queen: "This is a true friend, who understands our grief better than any of those who have come here." Then we went to have tea (I had had it half an hour before on the train, so I had coffee). Also there were the Empress of Russia[5], the new Queen[6], Princess Victoria[7] and the Kings of Denmark[8] and Greece[9]. Queen Alexandra, always so kind, talked a great deal about my dear mother. I also dined with Queen Alexandra, sitting next to her. The next day I went visiting with Soveral.

King Edward's funeral took place yesterday It was the most wonderful spectacle one could possibly see. I can't even try to describe it. Nine kings[10], more than sixty princes on horseback followed by their retinues; the Queens and Ladies in all the ceremonial carriages.

In the streets, where there were more than 4,000,000 people, the silence and respect were extraordinary. It was terribly hot; there were more than 6,000 cases of sunstroke. The ceremony in St. George's Chapel at Windsor was the most impressive one could imagine. I have no time to write any more, mother dear, it must wait till we are together again.

Confidentially, and only for your eyes, I must tell you that Soveral spoke to Queen Alexandra today In view of their conversation Queen Alexandra is to give a dinner party tomorrow, to which the family[11] in question" has been invited. We shall see how it goes. When you get this letter you will, God willing, already have received a telegram on the subject. How good it is of Queen Alexandra to think of all this in the midst of her tremendous grief ! May God help us !!!

Everybody here, and especially Queen Alexandra, Princess Victoria and the King, asks me to send lots of messages to my dear mother. All my staff respectfully kiss your hands. Many messages to all. With many loving thoughts - *saudades* - and infinite respect and love,
your (12) son kisses Your Majesty's feet
Manuel   London 21.V.1910"

1. The Infanta Eulalia (1864-1958) : youngest daughter of Queen Isabel II of Spain.
2. Soveral: Luis, Marquess de Soveral, G.C.M.G., G.C.VO. (1862-1922), Portugal's Foreign Minister 1895-7, Portuguese Envoy to the UK 1897-1910 ; Edward VII's friend, known in Society as "the Blue Monkey."
3. The King : King George V who had succeeded his father.
4. Queen Alexandra : widow of King Edward VII, formerly Princess Alexandra of Denmark.
5. The Empress of Russia : Dagmar, sister of Queen Alexandra and widow of Alexander III, Tzar of Russia
6. The new Queen : Queen Mary, King George V's consort, formerly Princess Mary of Teck.
7. Princess Victoria (1868-1935): unmarried daughter of Edward VII and companion to her mother.
8. The King of Denmark : Frederik VIII, eldest brother of Queen Alexandra.
9. The King of Greece: George I, chosen King of the Hellenes 1863 ; brother of Queen Alexandra and second son of Christian IX of Denmark.
10. Nine Kings : the others were Wilhelm II German Emperor,the deceased's nephew ; Haakon VII of Norway, son-in-law ; Ferdinand I of Bulgaria, second cousin ; Leopold II of Belgium, second cousin once removed ; Alfonso XIII of Spain, nephew by marriage ; see photograph page 50.
11. The family " in question" : The Fifes ?
12. This word is undecipherable in the Portuguese text of the letter, written on black-edged Buckingham Palace notepaper.

Acknowledgements:

Dom Manuel's own account of the Regicide is kept in the Torre do Tombo National Archives of Portugal and was printed in facsimile with a transcript and commentary text in 1990. Published in Lisbon by Alfa, the book is entitled *Diário de D. Manuel e estudo sobre o regicídio* and the author Miguel Sanches de Baêna has kindly approved of the reproduction of the King's sketch. George Lind-Guimarães, M.A.(Oxon), albeit an avowed republican (*sic*), has aptly translated Dom Manuel's poignant words.

Rocha Martins *Dom Carlos História do Seu Reinado* 1926 ;
　　　　　　　　Dom Manuel II História do Seu Reinado 1932
Serrão, Joaquim Verríssimo *Dom Manuel II* 1990
Professor Harold V. Livermore *A History of Portugal*
　　　　　　　　Cambridge University Press 1947

Rev Uick Loring, Parish Priest of St. James's Chuech, Twickenham
Thomas Devitt *The Parish of St.James, Twickenham, UK,* 1885-2008

Exmo Senhor Rui Pinto de Almeida Brave Ant, Multimedia Ltd DVD
Dom Manuel II o rei traido 2008
Professor Lionel Alves
Exmo Senhor Dom Pedro d'Avillez
Exmo Senhor Dr Paulo Lowndes Marques, O.B.E., Chairman of the British Historical Society of Portugal, for the choice of epithet for the memorial
Exmo Senhor Dr. António Costa de Albuquerque de Sousa Lara

John Crockford-Hawley, K.M.W.
Rev Robert Norwood, M.A.(Oxon). S.Th.(Lambeth)

Miss Margaret and Miss Pamela Davis, trustees of the
Urosevic Foundation, for a grant towards the printing costs

Malcolm Howe
31 King's Court North,
189 King's Road, Chelsea,
London SW3 5EQ

Epilogue:

When Queen Augusta left England she went to live with her new husband, Count Douglas, in Germany taking with her the contents of Fulwell Park. Miss Withers who accepted an invitation to stay was surprised to find the rooms in the new home furnished virtually the same as the corresponding rooms at Fulwell Park. Augusta outlived her second husband and died without any issue in 1966. In Geneva in May 1991, Sotheby's held a sale from the 'collection of King Manuel II of Portugal - the property of a Princely family', presumably the Hohenzollerns, including wedding presents, that realised over half a million pound sterling. In November 1992 in Lisbon there was a further sale of the personal property of the King and Queen, at the Palácio do Correio-velho. The following photographs are reproduced in the main from the auction catalogues, with acknowledgements.

Signed photograph of the Royal couple:

Augusta's signature was her nick-name *Mimi*.

Wedding presents:

Silver vase given by Prince Arthur, Duke of Connaught (brother of Edward VII) & his wife Princess Louise Margaret of Prussia

Rich edition. bound in enamelled silver, of the classic epic *Os Lusíadas* by Camões, given by the Portuguese emigrants in Galicia,

Silver-gilt cup given by Queen Alexandra inscribed *For my dear Manuel, King of Portugal, on his Marriage, from his affectionate 'Aunt' Alexandra*

The Royalist flag that flew over Vila Verde in 1912

The gold jewelled model of a *caravela* given by Portuguese Monarchists
now at Vila Viçosa

Dom Manuel with the Military Medical Regiment football team January 1917

Dom Manuel with wounded soldiers and their nurses at the entrance of a hospital

Dom Manuel with the staff of Alder Hey Military Orthopaedic Hospital 1917

Silver Art Nouveau plaque depicting the Archangel Michael conquering
the Devil given to His Most Faithful Majesty Dom Carlos I
by a Brazilian Foundation 1908

Design of the marble plaque for the Church of St James, Twickenham:

IN MEMORY OF
HIS MOST FAITHFUL MAJESTY
DOM MANUEL II
KING OF PORTUGAL
died 2nd JULY 1932
Fulwell Park aged 42
& QUEEN D. AUGUSTA VICTÓRIA
1890-1966
GODPARENTS OF MANY PARISHIONERS
BENEFACTORS OF THIS CHURCH
Na Glória de Deus
A Felicidade da Vida Eterna

End Cover: Dom Manuel II wearing his robes and insignia as a Knight of the Garter; photograph given to Exmo Senhor Dr. António Costa de Albuquerque de Sousa Lara, by his great-uncle, Dom António de Sousa Lara, and by whose inspiration the Foundation of the Order of St Michael of the Wing was established in the United Kingdom on 5th February 1984.